漢字字源入門

THE ORIGINS OF CHINESE CHARACTERS

王宏源　著

华语教学出版社　北京

SINOLINGUA BEIJING

First Edition 1993
Second Printing 1994
Third Printing 1997

To my mother
Guan Zongshuang

ISBN 7-80052-243-1
Copyright 1993 by Sinolingua
Published by Sinolingua
24 Baiwanzhuang Road, Beijing 100037, China
Printed by Beijing Foreign Languages Printing House
Distributed by China International
Book Trading Corporation
35 Chegongzhuang Xilu, P.O. Box 399
Beijing 100044, China

Printed in the People's Republic of China

目录 Contents

Chapter

INTRODUCTION

This book is intended as a guide to the origins and histories of Chinese characters. Although it could be used as a Chinese etymological dictionary, the book is an attempt to find a new way to teach the practical ideography of Chinese to those whose native scripts are alphabet-based.

Writing is a system of conveying ideas by means of conventional symbols that form visible marks. These symbols are traced, incised, drawn, or written on the surface of materials such as tortoise shells, bones, stone, metal, bamboo, papyrus, parchment, or paper. Writing gives permanence to human knowledge and enables communication over great distances.

Writing grows out of pictures. This is as it should be, since the most natural way of communicating visually is through pictures. At some remote time in the Upper Paleolithic period, perhaps about 20000 BC, early man in southern France and northeastern Spain drew sketches of his prey—horse, buffalo, deer and other animals—on the wall of his cave and colored them with earth and vegetable dyes. Several factors may have led to the creation of a primitive drawing, some aesthetic, some spiritual or magical. This may have been the beginning of art, but it was hardly the beginning of writing. Such pictures do not represent writing because they do not belong to a system of conventional signs and their significance can be understood only by the man who drew them or by his family and close friends who had heard of the event. However, genuine writing, whether it retains a pictorial form or not, serves purely to communicate.

In the process of using pictures to identify and recall objects or beings, a complete correspondence is established and gradually conventionalized between certain written signs and certain objects and beings. These simple pictures contain only those elements that are important for the communication of meaning and lack the embellishments that are included in an artistic representation. Since these objects and beings have names in spoken language, a correspondence is also established between the written signs and their spoken counterparts. When individual signs are used to express individual words and syllables, a consequence might be the development of a complete system of word signs; that is, word writing or so-called logography. In logography, one sign or a combination of signs expresses one word or a combination of words. However, pure logography is not found in any known system of writing. It exists normally only in conjunction with syllabography, as best represented in logo-syllabic writing.

Logosyllabic writing—that is, writing in which signs express words and syllables—is found in the Orient, the vast belt of Asia extending from the eastern shores of the Mediterranean Sea to the Western shores of the Pacific Ocean. Egypt and the area of the Aegean Sea, at least in the pre-Hellenic period, are included within the orbit of Oriental civilizations.

In this large area are found seven original and fully developed logosyllabic systems of writing: Sumerian in Mesopotamia, 3100 BC to AD 75; Proto-Elamite in Elam, 3000 to 2200 BC; Proto-Indic in the Indus Valley, around 2200 BC; Egyptian in Egypt, 3000 BC to AD 400; Cretan in Crete and Greece, 2000 to 1200 BC; Hittite in Anatolia and Syria, 1500 to 700 BC; and Chinese in China, 1300 BC to the present. Other logosyllabic system may at some time come to light, but at the present there are no likely candidates to be added to the above list of seven. The Proto-Armenian inscriptions discovered within the last few decades are too short and too little known to allow any safe conclusions. The mysterious Easter Island inscriptions are not writing even in the broadest sense of the word, as they are probably nothing but pictorial concoction for magical purposes. Finally, the systems of the Mayas and the Aztecs do not represent a full logosyllabic writing; even in their most advanced stages they never attained the level of phonographic development of the earliest stages of the Oriental systems.

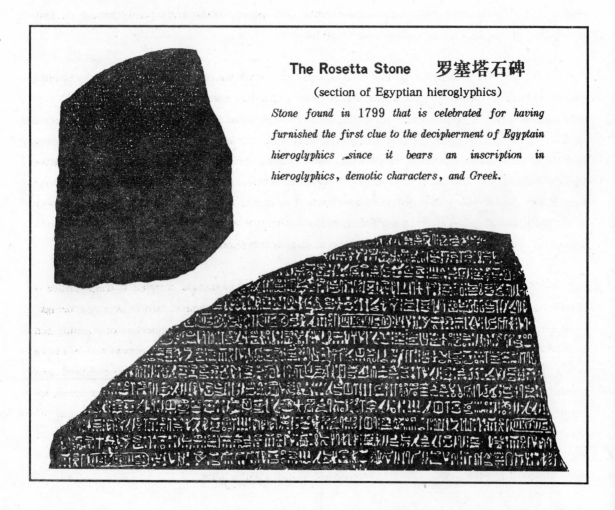

The Rosetta Stone　罗塞塔石碑

（section of Egyptian hieroglyphics）

Stone found in 1799 that is celebrated for having furnished the first clue to the decipherment of Egyptain hieroglyphics since it bears an inscription in hieroglyphics, demotic characters, and Greek.

Of the seven systems, three—namely, Proto-Elamite, Proto-Indic and Cretan—are as yet undeciphered. Consequently, modern understanding of the logosyllabic systems is limited to the remaining four systems: Sumerian, Egyptian, Hittite and Chinese. Chinese writing is the only logosyllabic writing system used today and it has developed a formidable degree of sophistication.

History does not throw much light on the beginning of Chinese writing. Chinese mythology attributes the invention of writing to Ts'ang Chieh (仓颉 cāngjié). It is said that he got his ideas from observing animals' footprints and birds' claw marks on the sand as well as other natural phenomena. When we try to fix in detail the developmental stages of the Chinese writing, there is a simple method to divide all Chinese characters into three stages, often overlapping chronologically: ideography, phonetic borrowing, and pictophonetic writing.

Ideography is the basic stage, the forerunner of writing. It consists of a drawing or a combination of drawings to represent the thing or action shown. The drawings are simplified and give a clear impression as a memory-aid device. Samples of these devices can be found all over the globe. The following Chinese ideographic characters are good examples: 木 mù stands for a tree; 鱼 yú for a fish, 虫 chóng for a snake, and 射 shè, literally "shoot", is the combination of a hand and the bow and arrow. The number of ideographic characters in Chinese writing system is limited. However, the surviving ideographs have static and definite meanings with simple but distinctive strokes. They are basic and easy to understand and many of them, especially the pictographs of single objects, are used as "radicals" in the Chinese writing.

Ideography is a natural method. But a complete system of ideographs have probably never existed either in antiquity or in modern times. To create and memorize thousands of signs for newly acquired words

Copy of a hieroglyphic Hittite inscription from the site of Carchemish (*after Renfrew, p.* 48).

赫梯语象形文字(卡尔凯美什遗址)。

Word-Signs On Potsherds　陶器上的刻划符号

上：西安半坡　下：临潼姜寨

仰韶文化（5000—3000 BC）

马家窑文化（3300—2500 BC）

and names is so impracticable that ideographic writing either can be used only as a very limited system, or it must be adapted in some new way in order to develop into a useful system.

Phonetic borrowing is the second stage. The number of function words and abstract nouns is very limited, but they are used frequently and difficult to draw or show. Therefore, signs for function words and abstract nouns were borrowed from ideographs with similar pronunciation. Such signs should also be simple and distinct. A borrowed character should have few strokes; and if the borrowed ideograph was not obsolete, it should be "returned" to its original meaning by adding an auxiliary element to distinguish the new character from its original borrowed pictorial form. These borrowed ideographs are called **phonetic loan characters (PLC)** in this book. The phonetic loan characters could be regarded as symbols. However, in many cases there is a tie of meaning between the original and borrowed forms. Let's see some examples:

北 **běi**, literally "north", is borrowed from an ideograph of two figures back to back. The "north" may derive from the fact that early man sat facing the sun to the south with his back to the north, thus 北 **běi** is a PLC. The word for "back" itself is returned as 背 **bèi**, adding a "human body" radical below.

自 **zì**, literally "self" and "from", is borrowed from the pictograph of a nose. Both "self" and "from" are difficult to express as drawings. Here, "self" may derive from a man pointing at his nose to express "himself", and the character was also adopted to indicate the abstract concept "from". 自 **zì** thus is a PLC. The word 鼻 **bí**, nose, is returned, includes the pictorial element 自 **zì** and a phonetic element 畀 **bì** below.

VI

Finally, 某 **dié**, meaning thin, derives from a pictograph of a tree with leaves, while 葉＝叶 **yè**, meaning leaf, has a plant-radical above. Note that since antiquity many of the pronunciations have changed, so that the original borrowed and returned forms no longer sound alike sometimes.

The adoption of the borrowing method in the Chinese writing system was a watershed between memory-aid picture writing and practical logo-syllabic writing. As the development of the society and the deepening of practice and realization, more and more objects and beings should be named precisely. Therefore, pictophonetic characters or pictophones emerged.

A pictophone consists of at least two parts: one part refers to the meaning of the character, and is usually called the "radical"; the other, the phonetic element, gives its sound. In most cases, the phonetic element also has meaning value as a "pictophonetic" element. The following examples are similar to rebus writing: 蝶 **dié** and 鰈 **dié**, literally butterfly and flounder, with the "worm" and "fish" radicals respectively, and the pictophonetic element 某 **dié**: thin. This stage is the last stage of development. Pictophonetic characters comprise about 90% of all Chinese characters. Today, the number of characters is fixed. When the Chinese need to introduce a word from the West, they use a new combination of characters to form a Chinese word such as 吉普 **jípǔ** for jeep, 浪漫 **làngmàn** for romance, 歇斯底里 **xiēsīdǐlǐ** for hysteria, 激光 **jīguāng**, or 镭射 **léishè** (in Taiwan) for laser.

Whether borrowed or created, a character generally begins its life in Chinese with one meaning and its ancient pronunciation. Yet no living language is static, and in time words develop a new pronunciations or meanings and lose old ones. However, the forms of the ideographic characters are somewhat static, especially the pictographs which derive the "letters" of Chinese from common objects or beings. This book will show you a panorama of these fascinating characters.

A look at the origins of the characters that make up the Chinese writing system involves also a look at the origins of the Chinese civilization. The early history of both China and the Chinese dates from the Neolithic period (about 5000 BC) to the Han Dynasty (206 BC to AD 220), including the Shang Dynasty (1523 to 1028 BC) and the Zhou Dynasty (1027 to 221 BC). By the Han Dynasty, the number and forms of common characters were fixed. Some illuminations and brief summaries of the ancient Chinese culture will help understand the ancient but practical ideographs as well as the remote civilization.

Etymology is not an exact science. Many times we are unable to discover the origin of a character, but more often there are ten origin stories for one character. Unproved but often ingenious etymological theories are put forward frequently, some plausible and attractive, some wildly improbable. I will choose the most likely explanations in this book, because the purpose of the book is not to introduce scholarly debates but to serve as a new way to learn Chinese characters.

A picture is worth one thousand words. The origins and histories of Chinese characters should be not a blind spot in the Chinese puzzle, but a key to resolving the puzzle.

Some Chinese characters have been simplified as *jianhuazi* (简化字), and these simplified forms are used on mainland China. But, the ancient form of Chinese characters must be referred to in such a book as this. And although the explanations for each entry are bilingual, they are not equivalent, the Chinese part being simpler with easy characters.

For transcription, the Chinese phonetic alphabet, or *pinyin* (拼音) as it is known, has been used with "four tones" (四声) in this book.

At the end of each article in this book, there are certain bracketed etymological and cross-referenced characters which are marked with *pinyin* and sometimes have a compact statement of the history of the given character.

Inscriptions

甲骨 "Shell and bone character" Inscriptions were carved on oracle bones with practical and angular strokes, Shang Dynasty.

金文 "Bronze character" Inscriptions are found on bronze vessels of the Shang and Zhou Dynasties. Bronze characters derive from prehistoric picture writing, and their lines are smooth yet forceful.

古文 "Ancient character" Inscriptions, which appear on the surface of bamboo, stone, pottery or ancient seals, were used mainly during the Warring States Period (475—221 BC).

篆文 "Seal character" A kind of standard or decorative character which appeared in the Qin Dynasty (221 —207 BC).

参考 "For reference"

H. Y. WANG

Dec. 1991

Chapter 1

MAN 人类

The first inhabitants on Chinese soil whose remains are known to us were the race to which Yuanmou Man belonged 1,700,000 years ago. However, Peking Man is more famous, and it was the focus of worldwide attention in 1927. Peking Man was later and more "human" than Java Man. Peking Man's bones were firstly discovered by Professor Pei Wenzhong at *Zhoukoudian* near Beijing. Unfortunately, all the *Zhoukoudian* hominid remains disappeared when being transferred from Peking to an American ship during the Japanese invasion of China prior to the Second World War. In Chinese characters, the form of a standing man means "great", perhaps because standing was a great feat in man's evolution.

中国大地上埋藏有十分丰富的古人类化石和旧石器时代遗物,至今已发现的早、中、晚各个时期的地点共 200 多处,包括直立人、早期智人、晚期智人各个阶段的人类化石。这当中据认为最早的为距今 180 万年的西侯度文化(山西省)和距今 170 万年的元谋人*(云南省)。1927 年裴文中教授在北京周口店发现的北京人则是最早发现,最具有影响的中国直立人。不幸的是,大量极其珍贵的北京人遗物,包括五个头盖骨和其它骨和牙齿标本在太平洋战争爆发前,全部在几个美国人手里弄得下落不明。

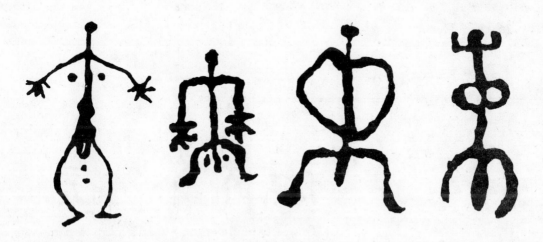

Figures in rock art (*after Gai, S. L.* 盖山林 (2) *fig.* 195; 765; 902; 908).

岩画中所见人形。

* 系根据古地磁学测定的数值。1983 年有人对此提出不同见解,认为元谋人化石年代不超过 73 万年,可能距今 50 至 60 万年。北京人距今 70 至 20 万年。

1.1 Man's Body 身体

rén
人

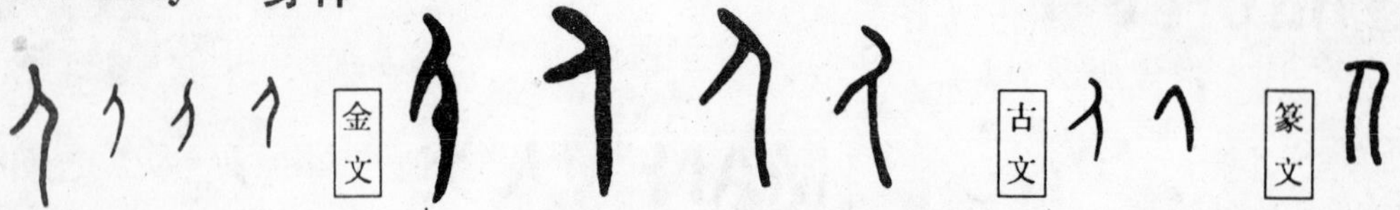
甲骨
金文
古文
篆文

—man, person

從＝从，苁，枞，cōng；從＝从，（丛＝叢）cóng；（众＝衆 zhòng；認＝认 rèn）.

* Drawing of a man, a figure in profile. The original form of 人 **rén** may reveal evolution from anthropoid apes to man. [亻 as radical]

人的侧视形。

tǐng
𡈼

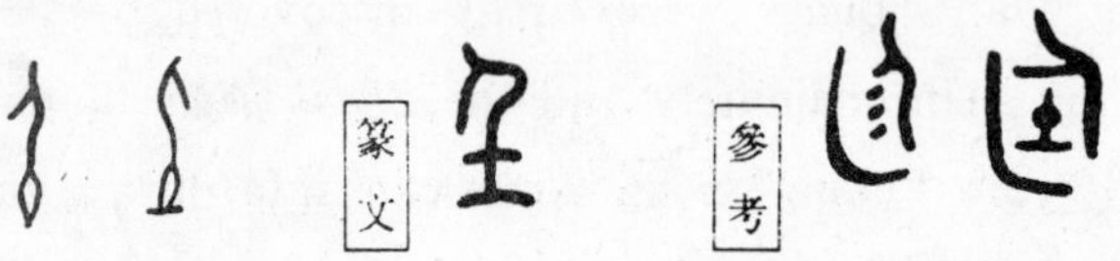
甲骨
篆文
参考
廷

—good; erect (archaic)

廷，庭，莛，蜓，霆 tíng；挺，艇，铤，梃 tǐng.

* Drawing of a man standing on land. 挺 **tǐng**: to erect; with a hand-radical which indicates a verb. [壬 rén, 人 rén, 土 tǔ: land]

人挺立于土上。

wù
兀

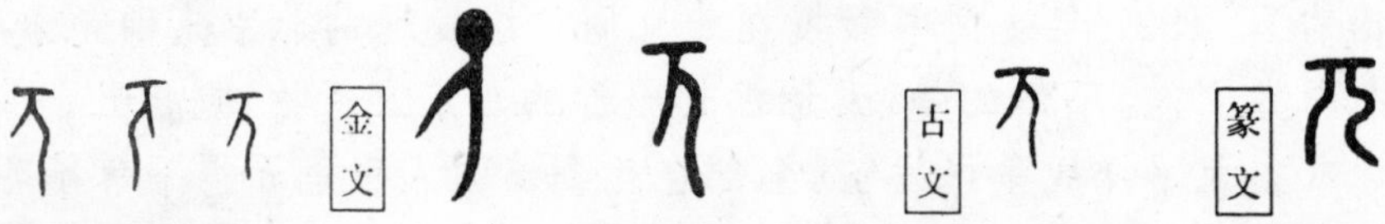
甲骨
金文
古文
篆文

—proud; upright; bald

阢 wù；堯＝尧 yáo；浇 jiāo；侥 jiǎo；挠，蛲，铙 náo；硗，跷 qiāo；翘 qiáo，qiào；娆，桡，荛，饶 ráo；绕 rǎo，rào；烧 shāo；骁 xiāo；晓 xiǎo.

* A derivative of 人 **rén** by adding a stroke on the man's head. [人 rén: man]

人上一横。

yuán
元

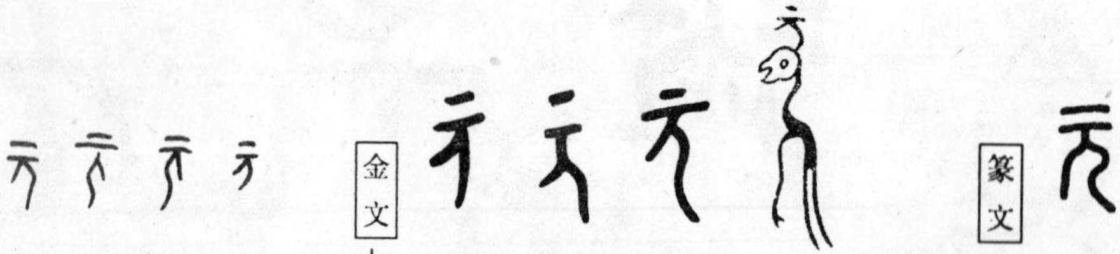
甲骨
金文
篆文

—basic, first, primary

阮 ruǎn；玩，顽，完，烷 wán；莞，皖，脘 wǎn；沅，鼋，（園＝园）yuán；（远＝遠 yuǎn）；垸，院 yuàn.

* Two strokes drawn on a man's head; a composite of the characters for "man" and "above". [上 shàng, 人 rén]

元字上从人头形，所以元即首（头）。元首二字重文迭义。

dà
大
—big, great
驮 tuó；（達＝达，鞑 dá）.

甲骨 大 大 大 大 大　金文 大 大　古文 大 公　篆文 大

* A standing man with his legs apart and his arms held out. See below.

人的正面形。"大"的字形中可引申出一种胯下形，表示控制、掌握等意，参见家、衣等字。

Nourlange rock painting, Northern Territory, Australia. 澳大利亚土著岩画。

tài
太
—greatest；too, over
汰，酞，钛，肽，（态＝態）tài.

甲骨 　金文 太　古文 太　篆文

* Shows one man placed over on another man. Later, the lower man was simplified as a dot. ［大 dà］

人胯下一点。古文字大太一字。

3

kàng

亢

— high, haughty; excessive, extreme

#伉, 抗, 炕 kàng; 杭, 吭, 航 háng; 沆 hàng.

* Derives from 大 dà: a standing man by adding a stroke between the person's legs. [大 dà]

亢为大的加划衍生字。

lì

立

— stand; set up; exist; at once

#粒, 笠 lì; 拉, 垃 lā; 啦 la; 泣 qì; 位 wèi; 翌, 翊 yì.

* Drawing of a man standing on land. [大 dà]

象人立于大地之上。

tiān

天

— overhead; sky; heaven, god; day, weather

#添 tiān; 忝, 舔 tiǎn; 吞 tūn.

* A standing man drawn to emphasize the head. [大 dà]

天即颠(头顶),强调"大(人)"的头部。

shēn

身

— body, life; personally

* A side view of a man's body depicting the arm, prominent belly with navel and phallus. 身 shēn is a radical that indicates the body or an action of the body. [殷 yīn]

象鼓腹的侧视人形。参考中所画为印第安人图形文字,意为"男人"。

nǔ

女

woman

\# 钕 nǚ；汝 rǔ；妆 zhuāng；好 hǎo.

* A modest woman squatting down with hands crossed in front of her body.

交手屈膝的女子形。

jǐ [篆文]

脊
—spine, backbone；ridge

\# 脊，嵴，瘠 jí.

* Drawing of a man's backbone and ribs. The lower part is a radical indicating a person's body. [肉 ròu]

脊字上部象人脊椎骨和肋骨形。

▶ The "X-ray" figure on a painted pottery plate, Banpo, the Neolithic.

半坡彩陶上的 X 光式人像。（采自《中国新石器时代陶器装饰艺术》,23 页,文物出版社,1982 年。）

wèi [金文]  [古文] [篆文]

胃
—stomach

\# 渭，猬，谓 wèi；膚＝肤 fū；喟 kuì.

* The upper part is said to be derived from a drawing of a stomach. The lower is a radical indicating a man's body. [田 tián, 肉 ròu]

胃字上面的"田"源于胃的象形。

xīn [甲骨] [金文]   [古文] [篆文]

心
—heart；feeling；center, core

\# 芯 xīn, xìn；沁 qìn；愛＝爱,暖,媛,瑗,暖 ài；蕊 ruǐ；憂＝忧,優＝优 yōu.

* A primitive anatomical representation of a heart. There are two radicals derived from this pictograph—a vertical one on the left side of a character；and a flat one written on the bottom of a character such as 恋 liàn and 慕 mù. Both of them are used in characters referring to emotions. [忄 , 小 as radicals]

象心形。心的部首有二种形式。在繁体字愛和憂中都用到了心。

yào 金文 **要**

—important; want to; must

#要：to ask, coerce, 腰 yāo.

* Ancient pictographs of 要 **yào** showed two hands placed to indicate the midsection of the body. PLC, 腰 **yāo**: waist, kidney; with the human body radical. According to Chinese tradition, the kidneys are the body's most important organs.

The second pictograph of 要 **yāo** portrays a woman being grasped by two hands, hence, the meaning "coerce". The upper middle part was an ancient phonetic element. Later, both the phonetic element and the hands merged in the character 西 **xī**. [女 nǚ]

要是腰的初文，象人双手叉腰以指示腰部，"腰乃一身之要"。

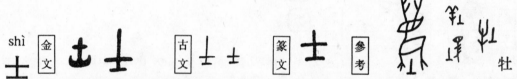

shì 金文 **士** 古文 篆文 参考 牡

— scholar-official; scholar, gentry; soldier; person

#仕 shì: to be an official.

* Drawing of a phallus. Or it derives from a drawing of an ancient weapon. PLC. [牡 mǔ: male (animal)]
象牡器之形。一说象古代兵器之形。

jí 甲骨 **吉**

— favorable omen, good luck; propitious, auspicious; good; a surname.

#佶，诘 jí; 髻 jì; 洁，结，诘，拮 jié; 桔 jú; 黠 xiá; 颉，撷 xié.

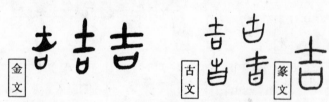

* A combination of 士 **shì** and a square. [士 shì]
吉字从士从口。

bǐ 比 甲骨 金文 古文 篆文

—to compare; liken to; ratio; next to

妣，吡，粃＝秕 bǐ；毖，狴，陛，庇，笓，（毕＝畢，毙＝斃）bì；批，砒，纰 pī；琵，枇，毗，蚍 pí；仳 pǐ；屁 pì.

* Shows two persons racing. [比 bǐ]
比象二人比赛竞走赛跑形。

bǐ 匕 甲骨 金文 篆文 参考 妣

—an ancient type of spoon

叱 chì；牝 pìn：female (animal).

* Derived and simplified from 比 bǐ. It is also a symbol for female, see below. PLC. [妣 bǐ：deceased mother，牡 mǔ：male (animal)]
匕是比字之省。

cǐ 此 甲骨 金文 古文 篆文

—this

雌 cí；疵 cī；柴 chái；砦 zhài；赀，訾，觜，髭，龇 zī；紫，啙，訾 zǐ；眦 zì；嘴 zuǐ.

* A combination of the symbol for female 匕 bǐ and a phonetic element 止 zhǐ. PLC, 雌 cí：female (animal), with the element of bird, 隹 zhuī. [雄 xióng：male, 匕 bǐ, 止 zhǐ]
此从匕止声。

yì 亦 甲骨 金文 古文 篆文

—also (literary form)

奕，弈 yì；迹 jì.

* Drawing of a man with two dots indicating the armpits. PLC. See below.
亦是腋字初文，用两点指示人的两腋，参见夜。

yè 金文 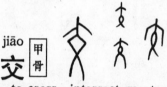 古文 篆文

夜
—night, evening
液, 腋, 掖 yè.

* A pictophone: 夕 xī, night, is the meaning element; 亦 yì, phonetic element. PLC, 腋 yè: armpit, with the human body radical. [亦 yì, 夕 xī, 肉 ròu]

夜夕意亦声。

jiāo 甲骨 金文 古文 篆文

交
—to cross, intersect; meet, join; hand over; acquaintance; mutual
郊, 茭, 姣, 蛟, 跤, 鲛, (胶＝膠) jiāo; 皎, 狡, 饺, 铰, 佼 , 绞 jiǎo; 较, 校 jiào; 效, 校 xiào; 咬 yǎo.

* Drawing of a man crossing his legs. [大 dà]

人两腿交互形。

běi 甲骨 金文 古文 篆文

北
—north
背 bēi: to carry on one's back; 背, 褙 bèi.

* Shows two people back to back. PLC, 背 bèi: to turn one's back on, the back of the body; with the human body radical. The Chinese emperor traditionally sat facing the sun to the south, with his back to the north. [人 rén, 匕 bǐ, 肉 ròu]

北为古背字, 作二人相背形。古人背北面南而坐。

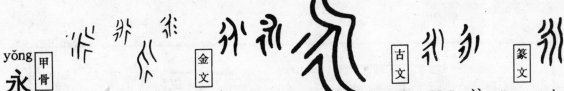

yǒng 甲骨 金文 古文 篆文
永
—perpetually, forever, always
泳，咏 yǒng.

* Depicts a man swimming. PLC, 泳 **yǒng**: swim; with an additional water radical. [水 shuǐ，人 rén，彳 chì]

象人水中游泳形。彳是一个表示动作的符号。

jié 甲骨 篆文
卩
—archaic character
叩 kòu: kowtow; (節 = 节 jiē, jié; 疖 jiē); 即 jì.

* Drawing of a kneeling or sitting man. [人 rén]

象人膝下跪形。古文字膝从卩。

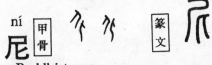

ní 甲骨 篆文
尼
—Buddhist nun
妮 nī; 妮，泥，呢，怩，铌 ní; 旎 nǐ; 泥，昵，伲 nì.

* Shows two people close together. PLC, 昵 **nì**: close, intimate; here the 日 rì, the sun, means warmth. [人 rén，尸 shī，匕 bǐ]

尼象两人相近的样子。

Clan insignias on bronze vessels.

1.2　Face　面部

西周人面玉饰

陕西沣西出土

Jade ornament with a face motif, West Zhou dynasty

---

xìn 篆文

—囟门 xìnmén：the boneless opening in a baby's skull.

＃恼＝惱，脑＝腦：brain，瑙 nǎo；思 sī：think，缌，锶 sī；鳃，腮 sāi；蕙 xǐ；细 xì.

* Drawing of a human skull.

人头颅形。

---

miàn 甲骨   篆文

—face; surface; aspect, side

＃麵＝面 miàn；湎，缅，腼 miǎn.

* Shows an attempt of drawing a man's face. ［目 mù：eye］

人面目形。

---

yè 頁＝页 甲骨 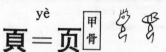 金文 古文 篆文 参考 须

—page；leaf

＃须 xū：heard, mustache；嚣 xiāo：clamor.

* A man drawn to emphasize the face. ［首 shǒu］

强调人首的人形。

shǒu 甲骨
首
—head; leader; first; a (song or poem)

#道 dào；導＝导 dǎo；憂＝忧 yōu；寡 guǎ.

* Shows an attempt of drawing a man's head, including the eye and the scalp. ［目 mù］
象人首形，上部为毛发。

yāo 甲骨
夭
—tender, young

#妖: seductively charming，夭 yāo；袄 ǎo；沃 wò；笑 xiào: laugh.

* Shows the actions of the head. As an element, it refers to facial expressions. ［大 dà］
人倾头形。

máo 金文
毛
—hair，feather，down；wool；a surname

#牦，旄，氄 máo；（笔＝笔 bǐ）；蚝 háo；耗 hào；尾 wěi；毳 cuì；撬 qiào；橇 qiāo.

* Drawing of a person's hair. ［长 cháng，手 shǒu］
人毛发形。

mù 甲骨
目
—eye

#苜，钼 mù；盲 máng；看 kàn；省 xǐng, shěng.

* Drawing of a man's eye. ［臣 chén］
象人的眼目之形。

jiàn 甲骨

見＝见

—to see; meet; opinion
#觅 mì; 蚬 xiǎn; 苋, 现 xiàn;
砚 yàn; (舰＝艦 jiàn).

金文   古文   篆文

* Drawing of a man who opens his eyes to see. Compare with 看 **kàn**: to look. [目 mù: eye, 人 rén: man]
象人目平视有所见。

gěn 篆文 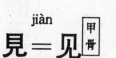 参考

艮

限

—One of the eight diagrams for divination used in *The Book of Changes* (《易经》).
#根, 跟 gēn; 痕 hén; 很, 狠
hěn; 恨 hèn; 腿 tuǐ; 退 tuì; 限
xiàn; 眼 yǎn; 银, 垠, 龈 yín.

* Drawing of a man looking back. [目 mù, 人 rén]
人回顾形。

tà 甲骨

罘

—(archaic character 目相及).
#懷＝怀 huái: to think of
(shedding tears onto clothes); 鳏
guān: widower (shedding tears
on fish—an emblem for women).

金文   篆文

* Picture of an eye shedding tears. [目 mù, 泪 lèi:
tear]
象垂泪的眼形。

zì 甲骨

自

—self, oneself; from; personal
#洎 jì; 咱 zán; 鼻 bí.

金文   古文   篆文

* Drawing of a nose seen from the front with nostrils
and a bridge. PLC, 鼻 **bí**: nose; pictophone, 畀 **bì**.
鼻形。自鼻古同字。

sì
四 [甲骨] [金文] [古文] [篆文]

—four

泗, 驷 sì.

* The number four, 四 sì, is borrowed from the drawing of the nostrils and the sound of breathing. PLC, 泗 sì: nasal mucus.

"四"字借鼻孔的形,鼻息的声。

kǒu
口 [甲骨] [古文] [篆文]

— mouth; opening; cut, hole; population

叩, 扣, 筘 kòu; 曰 yuē.

* Pictogram of a mouth with happy corners. As an element, 口 kǒu is borrowed to represent "speak" and "sound" which are difficult to depict. The square 口 kǒu is an important element, which generally appears in one of every five Chinese characters. In some ancient writings, the square also represented certain round things such as a pot, a melon or the head of a baby. But these "squares" were replaced with 日 rì or a triangle in order to avoid the confusion with the "mouth". [者 zhě, 瓜 guā, 子 zǐ, 保 bǎo, 或 huò]

象张开的嘴形。口是一个非常重要的汉字部件,主要用来表示语言和声音这类重要但不易用象形的方法表达的概念。在简化字中口出现的几率约为20%。由于书写的便利,在古文字中有一些近似为圆形的物体也用口来表示。但在现代汉字中则用日或三角形来表示这些物体,而避免过多使用口。

gān
甘 [甲骨] [古文] [篆文]

—sweet; willingly

绀 gàn; 柑, 苷, 泔, 柑, 疳 gān; 蚶, 酣 hān; 钳 = 拑, 箝 qián; 甜 tián.

* Depicts a mouth with something in it. [口 kǒu]
口中含物。

13

shé
舌

—tongue
敌 dí；颳＝刮，鸹 guā；聒
guō；话 huà；活 huó；括，蛞，
阔 kuò；适 shì；恬 tián.

* Drawing of a tongue protruding from a mouth. ［口
kǒu.］
象伸出口外的歧舌形。

qiàn
欠
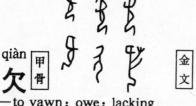
—to yawn；owe；lacking
吹，炊 chuī；坎，砍 kǎn；钦
qīn；饮 yǐn；歡＝欢 huān.

* Drawing of a man opening his mouth to yawn. ［人
rén，兄 xiōng］
象人张口打呵欠。

yán
言

— speech，word；to say，talk，
speak
唁 yàn；信 xìn；狺 yín；這
＝这 zhè，zhèi.

* The lower part of the character 言 yán is 口 kǒu：
mouth；the upper part derives from an ancient phonetic
element . See below.［讠 as radical，口 kǒu，音 yīn］
言从口辛(yǎn)声。

yīn
音
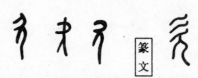
—sound；news，tidings；tone
暗，暗 yīn；谙 ān；暗，黯
àn；歆 xīn.

* 音 yīn and 言 yán are cognate characters.
音言同源字。

cì
次

— order, sequence; next; inferior, second-rate

＃茨，瓷 cí；盗 dào；羡 xiàn；资，姿，咨 zī；恣 zī.

duì 兑 甲骨 金文 古文 篆文

— one of eight diagrams for divination from *The Book of Changes* (《易经》); to cash (check).

＃锐 ruì；税，说 shuì；说 shuō；蜕 tuì；脱 tuō；悦，阅 yuè.

* Depicts a man sneezing. PLC. ［欠 qiàn］
象人张口打喷嚏。

* Shows a man opening mouth to speak. PLC，说 shuō：to say. ［人 rén，兄 xiōng，口 kǒu，八 bā］
兑表示人张口说话。

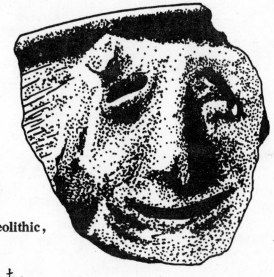

▶ A potsherd with a human face motif, the Neolithic, Shaanxi Province.

瓮口沿下堆塑人面像，仰韶文化，陕西扶风出土。

ěr 耳 甲骨 金文 古文 篆文

—ear

＃饵，铒，珥 ěr；弭 mí；聲＝声 shēng；茸 róng；闻 wén；聶＝聂，颞，镊，嗫，蹑 niè；摄，慑 shè；缉 jī；楫，辑，揖 jí；茸 qì.

* Drawing of a person's ear.
象耳形。

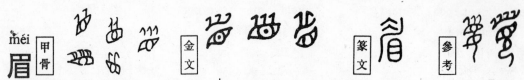

méi 甲骨 金文 篆文 参考

眉

—eyebrow

#湄,锏,猸,楣,鹛,嵋 méi；媚 mèi；蔑 miè；薨,瞢 méng；懵 měng；夢＝梦 mèng.

* Drawing of an eye with an eyebrow. ［目 mù］

象目上有眉毛形。

ér 甲骨 金文 古文 篆文

而

—moreover；and

耍 shuǎ；耐 nài：pondering about.

* The traditional explanation is that 而 ér was derived from a drawing of a beard. PLC. ［须 xū：beard and mustache］

下巴上的胡子。

yá 金文 古文 篆文 参考

牙

齿

—tooth；

#芽,蚜 yá；呀 ya；呀,鸦 yā；雅 yǎ；砑,讶,讶 yà；穿 chuān；邪 xié, yé.

* Portrays a pair of molars.

一对臼齿咬合形。

chǐ 甲骨 金文 古文 篆文

齿＝齿

—tooth；gear

#啮 niè：to gnaw.

* Drawing of frontal incisors. The upper part is a phonetic element，止 **zhǐ**. Later，the four teeth were replaced with one tooth in the simplified character. It is a radical. ［止 zhǐ，口 kǒu］

口中门齿形。"止"为声符。

1.3   Hands and Feet   手与足

▶ Handprints in rock painting (*after Gai, S.L.* 盖山林(1), *fig.* 760; 764).
岩画中所见手印。

1.3.1—Hands   手

shǒu 手 金文 古文 篆文

—hand

#掰 bāi：break off with the fingers and thumb；拜 bài；看 kàn.

* Drawing of a left hand with five fingers. In prehistoric cave or rock art, the painted hands were mostly left hands, since early artists usually used their right hands to paint, leaving only the left hands to copy. [扌 as radical, 毛 máo：hair]

象手之形。史前艺术中凡出现手的形象时多为左手,这是因为先民使用右手来画左手的形状。

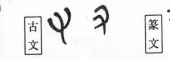

yòu 又 甲骨 金文 古文 篆文

—also, too

#驭 yù：to drive (a carriage)；友 yǒu：friend.

* Shows the right hand's action. PLC. In some characters the ancient form 又 **yòu** has been replaced by an alternate form , 寸 **cùn**. [右 yòu]

又表示右手及其动作。

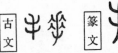

cùn 寸 篆文

—*cun*, a unit of length (= 1/3 decimetre)；very small, very short

* Derived from 又 **yòu**; and the short stroke or dot indicated the width of a finger, an ancient unit of length. Ten fingers' breadth equaled an ancient 尺 **chǐ**.

#村 cūn；忖 cǔn；衬 chèn；守 shǒu；狩 shòu；讨 tǎo；肘 zhǒu；绉 zhòu.

Today, the lengthes of *cun* , *chi* and *zhang* are approximately double their ancient value.

寸源于又。又下的短横表示一个手指的宽度为古代一寸的长度。见下面尺丈两字。

chǐ

—*chi*, a unit of lengt (=10 *cun*)
#（遟＝迟 chí）；咫 zhǐ: eight *cun* in Zhou Dynasty.

* Indicates a hand-span. Similar to the British who used the foot for measuring, early Chinese used the hand and arms to measure. The *chi*, one hand-span, is a basic unit of length. ［寸 cùn］

布手知尺，人手指拃开的长度为尺。

zhàng

—*zhang*, a unit of length (=10 *chi*); measure; man
#仗，杖 zhàng.

* The combination of 十 **shí**: ten and 又 **yòu**. 丈 **zhàng** meant ten hand-spans. ［尺 chǐ，又 yòu］

十尺（拃）之意。

bā

巴

—to hope earnestly; be close to
#芭，吧，笆 bā；吧 ba；把，钯，靶 bǎ；耙，爸 bà；肥 féi；葩 pā；杷，爬，耙，琶 pá.

* Drawing of the palm of a hand. The traditional explanation is that 巴 **bā** derives from the drawing of a boa. PLC.

巴象巴掌形。

bái

—write
#百，柏 bǎi；柏，伯，泊，舶，铂，箔，泉，魄 bó；啪 pā；帕，怕 pà；拍 pāi；珀，迫，粕，魄 pò.

* Drawing of a thumb. PLC.

象拇指之形。一说象人面貌之形。

18

dù
度 [篆文]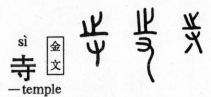
— limit; spend, pass; consideration; a unit of measurement for angles, temperature etc.; degree
#渡，镀 dù；度，踱 duó.

* The essential part of 度 dù is 又 yòu, the hand action. The hand was an important unit of measurement in China. 庶 shù without the bottom dots was the phonetic element of 度 dù. [庶 shù，又 yòu]

度字晚出，庶省声。又表示用手拊测量之意。

sì
寺 [金文] 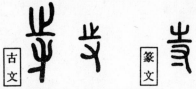 [古文] [篆文]
—temple
#持 chí；待 dài；等 děng；诗 shī；時＝时，鰣 shí；莳，侍，恃 shì；特 tè；峙，痔 zhì.

* A derivative of 又 yòu; its upper part 之 zhī contains both the phonetic and the meaning (stop) elements. Later, the 之 zhī was incorrectly substituted by 土 tǔ. PLC, 持 chí: to hold, grasp; with a hand-radical. [又 yòu，寸 cùn，之 zhī and 志 zhì]

寺是持的本字，"又"或"寸"为意符，上面的"土"源于"之"，为声符。

yù
舁 [篆文] [参考]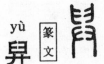
— (of two or more persons) to carry
#舆，輿＝与 yú；与，峿 yǔ；与，譽＝誉 yù；舉＝举 jǔ；興＝兴 xīng，xìng.

六 gǒng

* Shows two persons (four hands)carrying something together. Cf. 举 jǔ: to lift, raise, with a bottom hand-radical 手 shǒu. [又 yòu，共 gòng，兴 xīng]

象两人的四只手抬物。

fǎn
反 [甲骨] [金文] [古文] [篆文]
— to turn over; in the opposite direction
#返 fǎn；贩，畈，饭 fàn；扳 bān；阪，坂，板，钣，版，舨 bǎn；瓬 guī；叛 pài.

* Shows a hand climbing up a cliff. PLC. [扳 bān: pull，樊 fán，厂 hàn，又 yòu]

反象以手攀崖形。

zhǎo 甲骨　 金文　 篆文

爪
—claw, talon, paw
#抓 zhuā；爪 zhuǎ.

* Shows a hand grabbing something. It is a radical indicating grabbing, written at the top part of a character. PLC, 抓 **zhuā**: to grab, catch. [丑 chǒu, 又 yòu]

爪象人手形。

---

lì 甲骨　金文　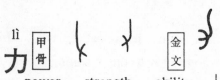 古文　篆文

力
— power, strength, ability, force.
#協＝协：to do sth. jointly, 脅＝胁 xié，(历＝歷 lì).

* Drawing of an arm. It is also said to be a drawing of an ancient plow. [又 yòu]

传统的解释为力象人手及臂形。一说力象耒形。掘土须用力。

---

yòu 甲骨　金文　 篆文　参考　
祐

右
—right
#佑：to help，祐：(of God) to bless, protect (family, people) yòu.

* Derived from 又 **yòu** by adding 口 **kǒu** as a symbol in order to distinguish from 又 **yòu**.

右源于又，古文字又右同字。

---

zuǒ 甲骨　金文　 古文　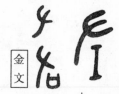 篆文　

左
—left
#佐 zuǒ；差 chā，槎 chá；差 chà；差 chāi；瘥 chài；差 cī；搓，磋，蹉 cuō；嵯 cuó；嗟 jiē；隋，隨＝随 suí；墮＝堕 duò；橢＝椭 tuǒ；髓 suǐ.

* Shows the left hand's action. 工 **gōng**, in the lower part of the character, is a symbol of a tool. PLC. [佐 zuǒ：an assistant；with a person-radical，又 yòu，工 gōng]

古左字表示左手。

zhēng 篆文  参考 静

争
—to contend, strive, dispute
挣，峥，狰，筝，睁，铮
zhēng；挣，诤 zhèng；净，静
jìng.

* Shows two hands contending for something. [爪
zhǎo, 又 yòu]
象两手争物形。

yuán 甲骨

爰
—then, therefore (literary);
援，媛 yuán；媛 yuàn；锾
huán；缓 huǎn；暖 nuǎn.

金文  古文 篆文

* Shows a person holding a stick to rescue another
person. PLC, 援 **yuán**：to pull by hand；help. [友
yǒu, 争 zhēng, 爪 zhǎo, 又 yòu, 手 shǒu]
象两人以物相援引形。

gōng 甲骨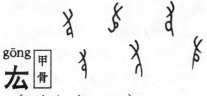

厷
—(archaic character)
宏，弘，泓 hóng；雄 xióng；
郄 qiè.

古文 篆文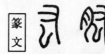

* The 厶 sī in the character shows a man's biceps.
PLC, 肱 **gōng**：the forearm；with a human body
radical. [雄 xióng：male, imposing, 宏 hóng：great]
字中的"厶 sī"指示人臂上的肱部。

dòu 甲骨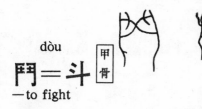

門 = 斗
—to fight

篆文

* Shows two people wrestling. [斗 dòu]
两人相斗。

chā 甲骨

叉

篆文

—fork, cross

#杈 chā；衩，叉 chǎ；汊，杈 chà；钗 chāi；蚤 zǎo；搔，骚 sāo.

* A hand, with the dots indicating the fingernails. [又 yòu, 蚤 zǎo：flea；with a worm-radical, 搔 sāo：to scratch (itch)；with a hand-radical]

叉字中的点指示手的指甲。

chǒu 丑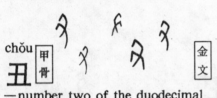

—number two of the duodecimal cycle; a clown

#妞 niū；扭，钮，狃，纽，钮 niǔ.

* Drawing of a claw. PLC. [又 yòu, 爪 zhǎo]

象爪之形。

fán 樊

—a surname; bird cage

#攀=矾 fán；攀 pān.

* Shows a man climbing a tree using two hands. The upper middle part is an ancient phonetic element. The lower part 大 **dà** derives from a depiction of both hands. PLC, 攀 **pān**：climb；with a bottom radical of 手 **shǒu**：hand. [林 lín：forest]

用双手攀爬树木。

1.3.2—Feet 足

zhǐ 止

—to stop；only

#址，芷，趾，沚 zhǐ；扯 chě；企 qǐ；志 zhì；寺 sì；齿 chǐ.

* Drawing of a footprint. PLC, 趾 **zhǐ**：foot, toe.

象人足或足趾形。

▶ An inscription of foot on a pottery fragment, Shang period.

陶文·止。商代。

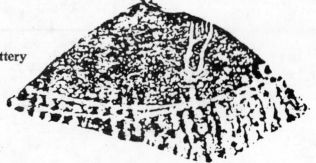

zhī 之
—of
#芝 zhī.

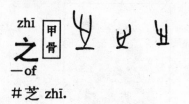 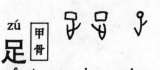 

* A derivative of 止 zhǐ with an additional stroke below. It was borrowed to be a function word. ［止 zhǐ］

之是止的加划衍生字。从止从一，表示人所至。

zú 足
—foot; enough, ample
#促 cù; 捉 zhuō; 龊 chuò.

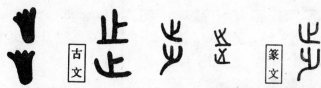

* A footprint. The upper square could be supposed as a symbol to distinguish with 止 zhǐ. ［正 zhèng, 止 zhǐ, 疋 pǐ］

足字下部为足形或足趾形。上部的口指代城邑。正足古同字。

bù 步
— step, pace, stage; to go on foot
#频 pín; 涉 shè; 陟, 骘 zhì.

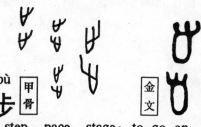

* A pair of footprints. Note the "big toes" of the footprints. ［止 zhǐ］

一对足印形。

zǒu 走
—to walk, go
#陡 dǒu; 徒 tú.

奔

* Drawing of a man walking, swinging his arms. The upper part 土 tǔ derives from the drawing of a walking man. There is a symbol of a footprint under the walking man. Compare with 奔 bēn：to run quickly, with three footprint symbols under a running man. It is interesting to note that a trend in modern art portrays motion by using repeated forms, such as Marcel Duchamp's *Nude Descending a Staircase*, *No.* 2. ［大 dà, 止 zhǐ］

象人摆臂行走形。

1.4　From the Womb to the Tomb　人的一生

▶ Fuxi and Nüwa, the primordial ancestors of China.
Rubbing of a stone from a tomb, Han Dynasty (*after Wang, D.Y.*).

伏羲女娲图。汉代，南阳画像砖。

bāo 包

— to wrap up; to include; package; a bun

＃苞，炮，孢 bāo；雹 báo；饱 bǎo；抱，刨，鲍 bào；泡 pāo；炮，刨，咆，庖，袍 páo；跑 pǎo；泡，炮，疱 pào.

* Shows a baby in its mother's womb. PLC, 胞 bāo: womb, the placenta of a child. ［孕 yùn: to be pregnant, pregnancy］

象在母亲腹中的胎儿形。

sì 巳

—the sixth of the twelve Earthly Branches

＃汜，祀 sì.

* A human embryo. PLC. (Compare 巳 sì with 己 jǐ and 已 yǐ.) ［包 bāo，子 zǐ］

象胎儿形。

yí 台

—I; happy (archaic)

＃怡，贻，饴，诒 yí；冶 yě；治 zhì；臺＝台，抬，鲐，炱，邰，骀，苔 tái；胎，胎 tāi；笞 chī；始 shǐ；殆，怠，迨，骀 dài.

* The combination of ㄙ sī and 口 kǒu. ［以 yǐ，胎 tāi: embryo，始 shǐ: beginning］

台 (从ㄙ) 从口以声。

24

育（毓） yù 甲骨 金文 篆文

— to give birth to; to rear, raise, bring up; education

毓 yù；流，硫，琉，旒，锍，鎏 liú；梳，蔬，疏 shū.

* Depiction of childbearing. The baby is inverted and the dots represent amniotic fluid. 毓 yù is the ancient form of 育 yù. [每 měi, 肉 ròu, 子 zǐ]

育（毓）象妇人生下婴儿形。婴儿出生时头先出现，故育（毓）字中婴儿头向下方。毓字中"倒子"下方的点代表分娩时流出的羊水。

后 hòu 甲骨 金文 古文 篆文

—queen

逅 hòu；骺 hóu，垢，诟 gòu.

* Derives from 毓 yù, see above.

古文字中，后毓同字。

衣 yī 甲骨 金文 古文 篆文

—clothes, coating; afterbirth

依，铱 yī；裔 yì；哀，镺 āi；亵 xiè.

* Perhaps the drawing depicts the essential part of the human afterbirth. According to the traditional explanation, this character is a picture of an ancient jacket. It is a radical for garments. [衤 as radical, 大 dà]

衣字下部可能指衣胞。传统的解释为衣象襟衽左右掩覆之形。

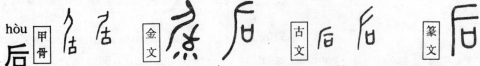

初 chū 甲骨 金文 篆文

—at the beginning of; first (in order); original; a surname.

* Shows a knife severing the umbilical cord. [刀 dāo：knife，衣 yī：afterbirth]

初表示用刀割断脐带。

zǐ

子

—son, child

#好 hǎo；孕 yùn；仔，籽 zǐ；

仔 zī；字 zì.

* Shows a baby wrapped in swaddling clothes with two arms free. (Cf. 字 **zì**: to give birth to (archaic); the upper radical derived from 大 **dà**.)

象在襁褓里的婴儿。

ér

兒 = 儿

—son

#倪，霓，猊，鲵 ní；睨 nì.

* A traditional explanation says that 儿 **ér** shows the boneless opening in a baby's skull. [囟 xìn, 人 rén]

象小儿头大而囟门未合之形。

kǒng

孔

—hole, aperture; a surname

#吼 hǒu；乳 rǔ；芤 kōu.

* Shows a baby sucking the breast. [乳 rǔ: milk, breast; 爪 zhǎo]

孔可能源于婴儿吮(shǔn)乳之形。

bǎo

保

— to protect, defend; to keep, maintain; to ensure.

#葆，堡，褓 bǎo；煲，褒 bāo.

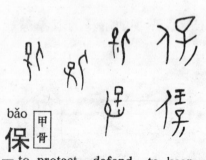 

* Shows a man carrying a baby on his back. [人 rén, 子 zǐ]

象人负子形。

nǎi
乃 甲骨  金文 古文 篆文
—to be (written)
#奶，艿，氖 nǎi；薾 nài；仍 réng；扔 rēng；孕 yùn；秀 xiù.

* A simple depiction of breast. PLC，奶 nǎi：breast, milk.

象妇女乳房侧面形。

mǔ
母 甲骨 金文 古文 篆文
—mother；female
#姆，拇 mǔ；毒 dú.

* Drawing of a mother during her breast-feeding period. Two dots marking the breasts in the character 母 mǔ are the only differences that distinguish the two characters 母 mǔ and 女 nǚ from each other. [女 nǚ，每 měi]

在"女"胸部加上表示女乳的两点构成母字。

fū
夫 甲骨 金文 古文 篆文
—man；husband
#跌，呋，（肤＝膚），麸 fū；扶，芙，蚨 fú.

* Portrays a man with a hairpin in his hair. The hairpin was a sign of ritual initiation. [大 dà]

男子戴发簪形。发簪是接受成人礼的标志。

▶ **Rock painting · Copulation**
(*After Gai, S. L.* (1) *fig.* 873, 877；(2) *fig.* 1412.)

岩画·交媾图。

bó

孛 —comet

\# 勃，脖，渤，鹁 bó；饽 bō；
孛，悖 bèi；荸 bí.

* A combination of 子 **zǐ** and 丰 **fēng**. Or a comet with its tail and coma. [子 **zǐ**]

从子、从丰，是孩子蓬勃向上的形声兼会意字。

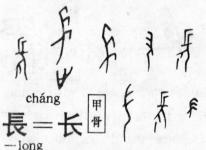

cháng

長＝长 —long

\# 张 zhāng；怅 chàng；伥 chāng；长：elder，涨 zhǎng；帐，胀，涨 zhàng.

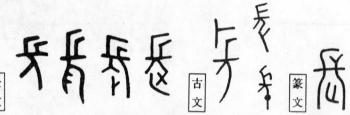

* A person with long hair. [毛 **máo**，人 **rén**，髟 **biāo**: a radical referring to hair or hairstyles]

象人长发之形。后在字形中加杖以示长（zhǎng）者。髟，头发长貌。

lǎo

老 —old (in age); become old

\# 佬，姥，铑 lǎo；耊 dié.

* Shows an old man leaning on a stick. See below.

象老者倚杖形。

kǎo

考 — deceased father or grandfather; to test, examine; investigate

\# 烤，拷，栲 kǎo；铐 kào；號=号 háo, hào；巧 qiǎo.

* Derives from 老 **lǎo**, but with a different stick. "丂" is the "stick" in the character. [老 **lǎo**，朽 **xiǔ**: decayed, senile]

老人手拄拐杖形。老考二字同源。

xiào
孝
—filial pierty; mourning

#哮 xiāo；教 jiāo；教，酵 jiào.

* Shows an old man supported by his son. [老 lǎo：old, 子 zǐ：son]

象子扶侍老者之形。

shòu
壽＝寿
— a person's age; birthday celebration; something burial or having to do with burial

#筹，俦，畴 chóu；祷 dǎo；涛 tāo；铸 zhù.

* The upper part of 寿 shòu is a drawing of an old man, and the bottom shows a hand holding a wine vessel. The middle part was an ancient phonetic element. See above. [寸 cùn]

手持酒器向老者祝寿形。寿从老畴声。

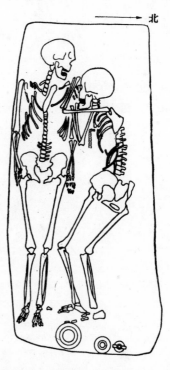

北

0   50厘米

▶ A man and a woman buried close together, the woman's skeleton is semi-flexed. The Neolithic, Gansu Province.

男女合葬墓（甘肃永靖秦魏家 M105）。齐家文化，新石器时代。（采自《新中国的考古发现和研究》，124 页。）

29

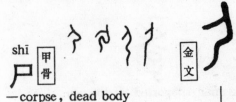

shī 甲骨 / 金文 / 篆文

尸
—corpse, dead body

* Shows a man bending his knees. 尸 **shi** is a radical referring to a person's action. [人 rén, 歹 dǎi]

象屈膝的人形。本来是对东尸(夷)的贱称。

xiān 甲骨 / 金文 / 古文 / 篆文

先
—earlier, before, first
酰 xiān；跣, 铣 xiǎn；(宪=
憲 xiàn)；洗, 铣 xǐ；(选 = 選
xuǎn).

* The ancient form of 先 **xiān** is a combination of a man and an upward footprint, indicating a forefather who has passed away. [止 zhǐ, 人 rén]

先从止在人上，表示逝去的先祖。

jiàng 甲骨

降
—to fall, move to a lower place
绛 jiàng；降 xiáng：to
vanquish, surrender.

金文 / 古文 / 篆文

* Borrows two downward footprints to represent a man descending a ladder or stairs. The right part, the two footprints, is an element in certain characters. [阜 fù, 止 zhǐ, 步 bù]

用在石阶边的两个指向下方的足印表示下降的动作。

30

Chapter 2

NATURE 自然

2.1 Mother Nature 大自然

▶ A bird in the sun. Rubbing of a brick
from a tomb in Henan. Han Dynasty.
东汉画像砖·太阳鸟。河南南阳出土。

rì

— sun; day

＃ 晶 jīng；昌，猖，娟，菖，鲳
chāng；唱，倡 chàng.

＊ Drawing of the sun. The dot in the sun stands for
sunshine, not a sunspot.   〔口 kǒu：mouth and 月
yuè：moon, month〕

象太阳形，中间一点表示日光。

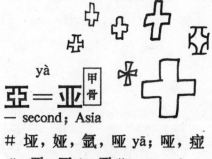

yà

— second; Asia

＃ 垭，娅，氩，哑 yā；哑，痖
yǎ；恶，垩 è；恶 ě, wū, wù.

＊ The early Chinese believed that the earth was square
and the sky was round. 亚 yà indicates the square earth
with its four corners occupied by pillars. These pillars
were said to prop up the sky.

亚字可能源于中国人"天圆地方"的观念。亚指
方形的地，但四个角被支撑苍天的柱子占用去了。

31

dàn
旦 甲骨
— dawn, morning
蛋，但，（担＝擔）dàn；（胆
＝膽），疸 dǎn；（担 dān）；祖，
坦，钽 tǎn.

* A depiction of sunrise.   ［日 rì，丁 dīng］
日出。古文字从日，丁声。

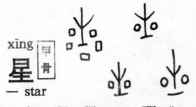

xīng
星 甲骨
— star
惺，猩，腥 xīng；醒 xǐng.

* The ancient form of 星 xīng was a drawing of a cluster of stars with the phonetic element 生 shēng. ［晶 jīng：brilliant, glittering］
象天上的群星，生为声符。

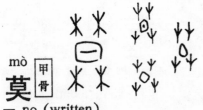

mò
莫 甲骨
— no (written)
漠，寞 mò；摸 mō；摹，模，
膜，馍 mó；模 mú；募，墓，
幕，暮，慕 mù.

* The ancient form of 莫 mò showed the sun setting in the woods. Later, the "forest" symbol was replaced by a grass-radical. PLC, 暮 mù：dusk, evening；with a lower sun-radical.   ［林 lín：forest，日 rì：sun，草 cǎo：grass］
日落林木草丛中。

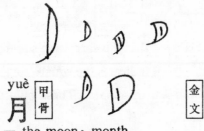

yuè
月 甲骨
— the moon；month
刖 yuè；（钥＝鑰 yào，yuè；
阴＝陰 yīn).

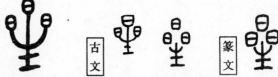

* Drawing of the moon, a new moon. ［日 rì，夕 xī］
象半月之形。

夕 xī 甲骨  金文 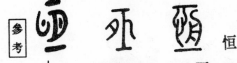 古文   篆文

— sunset, evening

汐，穸，矽 xī.

* 夕 xī is the original form of 月 yuè：moon. Later, the dot in the moon disappeared. PLC.

夕是月的本字。后省去点以与月相区分。

亘 gèn 甲骨  参考  恒

— to extend, stretch

恒 héng： permanent, perseverance；宣 xuān；垣 yuán.

* Ancient forms of 亘 gèn showed the moon between two strokes indicating its waxing and waning phases. Or the middle 〞日 rì〞 derives from a boat, thus, the two horizontal strokes represent the banks. PLC.
[月 yuè, 舟 zhōu]

亘表示月亮圆缺的变化。

明 míng 甲骨 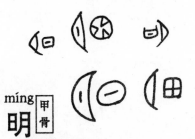 金文

— bright; clear

盟 míng；盟，萌 méng.

* The traditional interpretation is that 明 míng is a combination of the sun and the moon. Perhaps 明 míng recorded a prehistoric supernova observed near the lunar crescent. [日 rì, 月 yuè]

明的古文以及甲骨文中一些写法都是从日从月。或从窗从月，会月光照进窗户而光明意。

名 míng 甲骨   金文 古文 篆文

— name；fame, reputation；famous

茗，铭 míng；酩 mǐng.

* A combination of 夕 xī and 口 kǒu.
[夕 xī, 口 kǒu]

名从口从夕，表示夜间（夕）看不清对方的面孔，而询问或自报姓名的意思。

雲 = 云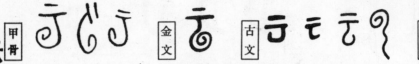

yún

— cloud

芸, 耘, 纭 yún; (运 = 運, 酝 = 醞 yùn); 魂 hún; 昙, 坛 = 壇 tán.

* A cirrus cloud. The upper part, the two short strokes, is the ancient form of 上 **shàng**: upper, implying the sky.　[上 shàng]

象回转的云形。上面两横表示上空。

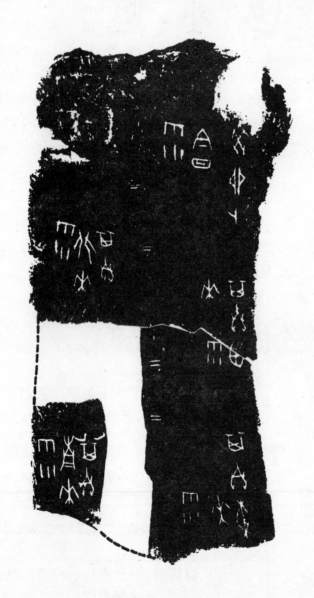

◀ Inscriptions on an oracle bone: *Today it will rain. Is the rain coming from the west? the east? the north? or the south?* (*After Kuo Mo-jo* (2).)

卜辞：癸卯卜，今日雨？其自西来雨？其自东来雨？其自北来雨？其自南来雨？

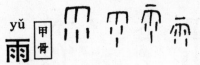 

yǔ
雨 [甲骨]
— rain
漏 lòu：to leak.

* Shows rain pouring from the sky. It is an upper radical for many characters denoting certain types of natural phenomena.

象雨点自天而降之形。

 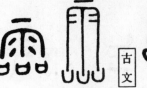

líng
零 [甲骨]
— (rain) fall; zero
靈＝灵，棂，鄮 líng.

* The combination of 雨 yǔ：rain and 口 kǒu：the sound of rain, thus, it was borrowed to indicate 零 líng：zero. The lower 令 lìng is a later addition of phonetic element.　〔雨 yǔ，口 kǒu，令 lìng〕

从雨从口令声，雨落下的声音。

shēn
申 [甲骨]
— to state, express; the ninth of the twelve Earthly Branches; a surname.
伸，呻，绅，砷 shēn；神 shén；（审＝审 shěn）；畅 chàng.

* An attempt to draw a bolt of lightning. PLC，電＝电 diàn：lightning, electricity；神 shén：god, divinity.

象闪电形。引申为神灵。

léi
雷 [甲骨]
— thunder
擂，镭，累 léi；累，蕾，傫 lěi；擂，累 lèi；螺，骡 luó.

* Ancient forms of 雷 léi depict lightning accompanied by peals of thunder. Later, the symbols for thunder were reduced to three 田 tián, which was topped with the radical for rain. The modern 雷 léi is simplified with one "田".　〔申 shēn，雨 yǔ〕

雷古字形从申从雨，(三个)"田"是声符。

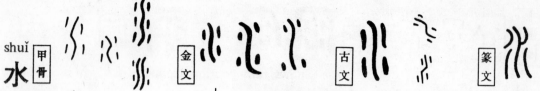

shuǐ 水 甲骨 金文 古文 篆文

— water; river

＃ 尿 niào, suī：urine; 氽 cuān.

* A stream with four dots representing the drops of water or pebbles on its bank.　［氵 as radical］

象溪水形，四点表示水滴。

qì 气 甲骨 金文 篆文

— gas；air；breath；smell, odour

＃ 乞 qǐ；汽，迄，讫 qì.

* Shows clouds in thin parallel layers or vapor on the surface of a lake. PLC, 汽 qì：steam, vapor.

象云层或水面蒸气形。

chuān 川 甲骨 金文 古文 篆文

— river

＃ 氚 chuān；钏 chuàn；顺 shùn；巡，驯 xún；训 xùn；圳 zhèn.

* A river.

河川形。

huí 回 甲骨 金文 古文 篆文

— circle；to return, go back

＃ 洄，茴，蛔 huí.

* Shows a whirlpool or eddy. PLC, 洄 huí：(of water) whirl.

象水回流形。

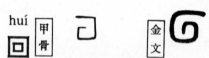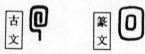

zhōu 州 甲骨 金文 古文 篆文

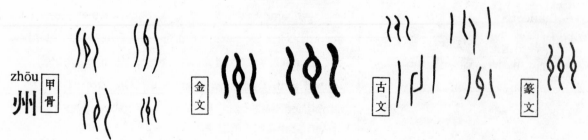

— an administrative division (ancient)

洲 zhōu；酬 chóu.

* Depicts an island in the middle of a river.

象河心小岛形。

quán 泉 — spring

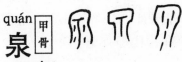

* Shows spring water flowing from a cave or from the mouth of a spring.　[水 shuǐ，原 yuán]

泉水从泉眼或山洞里流出。

腺 xiàn：gland.

yuán 原 — original；unprocessed；to excuse，pardon；plain；a surname

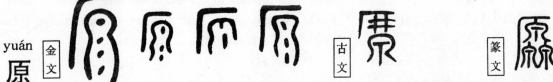

* Shows a spring flowing from the face of a cliff. PLC，源 yuán：fountainhead；source.　[厂 hàn，水 shuǐ，泉 quán]

泉水从山崖边流过。原为源字初文。

源，螈 yuán；愿 yuàn.

shān 山 — mountain，hill；a surname

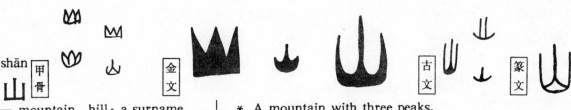

* A mountain with three peaks.

象山峰并立之形。

舢 shān；疝，汕，讪 shàn；（灿＝燦 càn）.

qiū 丘 — mound，hillock，dune；a surname

* Two mounds of dirt.

两丘突起形。

邱，蚯 qiū；岳 yuè.

37

hàn   金文 古文 篆文

厂

— river bank; cliff-dwelling (archaic)

（厂 = 厂 chǎng.）

* A cut bank. PLC, 岸 àn: river bank, coast; with the mountain-radical and the phonetic element 干 gàn. 厂 hàn is a radical for rocks and cliffs.

象河岸形。传统的解释为山石崖岩形。

---

shǎo 甲骨 金文 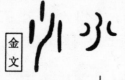 古文 篆文

少

— few, little, less

少 shǎo；抄，钞 chāo；吵，炒 chǎo；杪，眇，秒，渺，缈 miǎo；妙 miào；挲 sa；沙，砂：grit，纱，裟，鲨 shā；娑，挲 suō；劣 liè.

* The four dots in the drawing may represent sand. PLC, 沙 shā: sand; with a water-radical implying the location of the sand.

少从四点。

---

xiǎo 甲骨 金文   篆文

小

— small

雀 què，qiāo；（尘 = 塵 chén）；尖 jiān；肖 xiào；肖，消，逍，宵，霄，硝，削，销 xiāo.

* Three dots. ［少 shǎo］

小从三点，从少省。

2.2 Flora 植物

mù 甲骨 金文  古文 篆文

木

— tree；wood

沐 mù；林 lín；森 sēn.

* Pictograph of a tree with its branches and roots shown. It is a radical.

象树形。

zhū 朱

— vermilion, bright red; cinnabar, a surname

\# 侏，珠，株，诛，铢，蛛 zhū；殊，姝 shū.

* The dot（later a horizontal stroke）indicates the trunk of a tree. PLC, 株 zhū：stem of a plant.

［木 mù：tree，干 gàn］

木中间加指示符号圆点，是株的初文。

běn 本

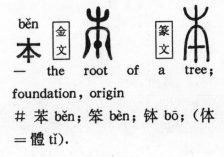

— the root of a tree; foundation, origin

\# 苯 běn；笨 bèn；钵 bō；(体 ＝體 tǐ).

* The roots of a tree emphasized by an additional short stroke near the base of the character.　［木 mù］

本字下面的短横用来表示树的主根。

mò 末

— end; minor details

\# 沫，抹，茉，秣 mò；抹 mǒ，mā.

* Constructed like 本 běn（above），末 mò shows the branches of a tree emphasized by a short stroke on the upper part of the character.　［木 mù，未 wèi］

用一短横指示树木枝干的末端。

wèi 未

— the eighth of the twelve Earthly Branches；to have not

\# 味 wèi；妹，昧，魅，寐 mèi.

* Derived from 木 mù. It was "borrowed" to be used as one of the twelve Earthly Branches in the duodecimal cycle for counting time. ［木 mù，末 mò］

未象木重枝叶形。

shēng
生
— grow
牲，笙 shēng；眚 shěng；胜 shèng；旌 jīng；性，姓 xìng.

* A seedling growing on land.
象草木生出地面形。

duān
端
— beginning; extremity
揣 chuāi；踹 chuài；喘 chuǎn；端 duān；瑞 ruì；湍 tuān；惴 zhuì.

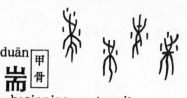

* A seedling breaking through the soil.
[才 cái，不 bù，而 ér]
象小苗破土而出。

cǎo
草
— grass

* Pictograph of grass. 早 **zǎo** is a phonetic element. The upper part is an important radical for grasses and plants. [艹 as radical，早 zǎo]
草是形声字。上部草字头是一个部首。

dié
葉
— thin (archaic)
蝶，碟，谍，堞，揲，喋，蹀，牒，鲽 dié；葉＝叶 yè.

* A tree with its leaves shown. This character is a common element, with the meaning "thin". PLC，葉 ＝叶 yè：leaf；with an upper plant-radical.
[木 mù，世 shì]
象树有叶形。

cái
才

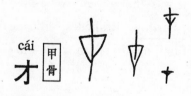

— ability, talent, gift; people of a certain type; simplified form of 纔：just; only

\# 材，财 cái；闭 bì；豺 chái；在 zài；存 cún.

* The traditional interpretation is that 才 **cái** is a depiction of a germinating seed breaking through the soil. PLC.

种子胚芽出土形。

bù 甲骨
不
— not
\# 钚 bù；杯 bēi.

* The root of a germinating seed. PLC. See below.

种子萌芽时的胚根形。

pī 金文 古文 篆文
丕
— big, great (written)
\# 邳，坯 pī；呸，胚 pēi；苤 piě.

* With the addition of a single bottom stroke, 丕 **pī** is a derivative of 不 **bù**. PLC, 胚 **pēi**：embryo.

[不 bù, 肉 ròu]

丕为不的加划衍生字。

Stages in the germination of a corn seed.
玉米种子萌芽示意图。

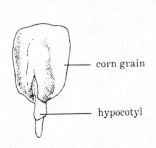

corn grain

hypocotyl

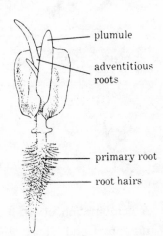

plumule

adventitious roots

primary root

root hairs

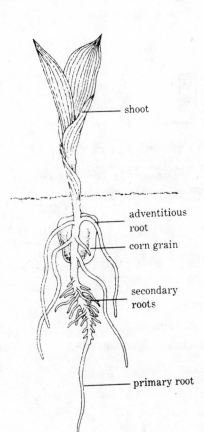

shoot

adventitious root

corn grain

secondary roots

primary root

Flowers

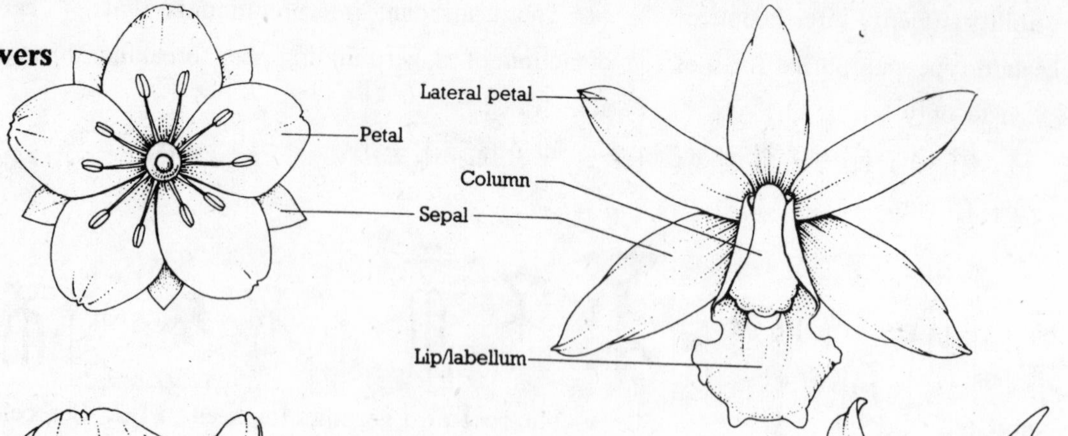

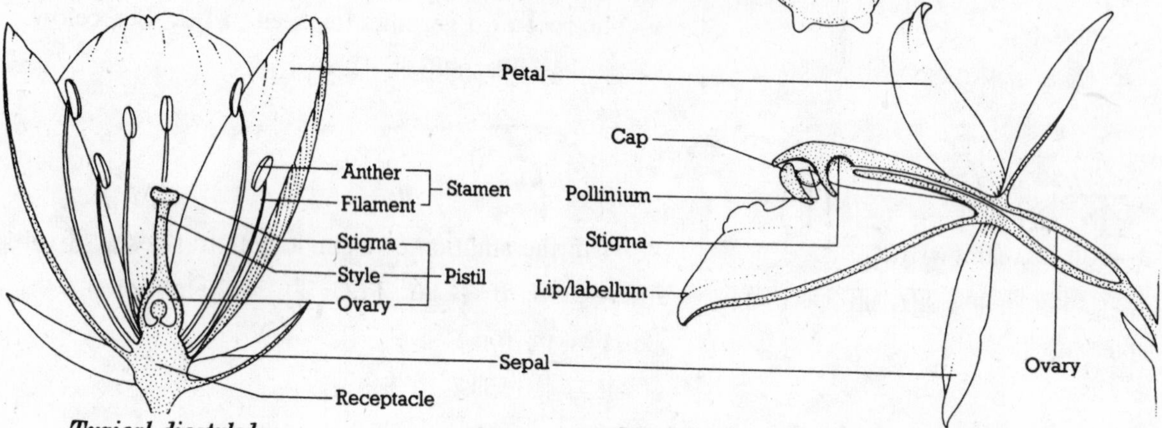

Typical dicotyledon

Specialized monocotyledon (orchid)

tún

屯

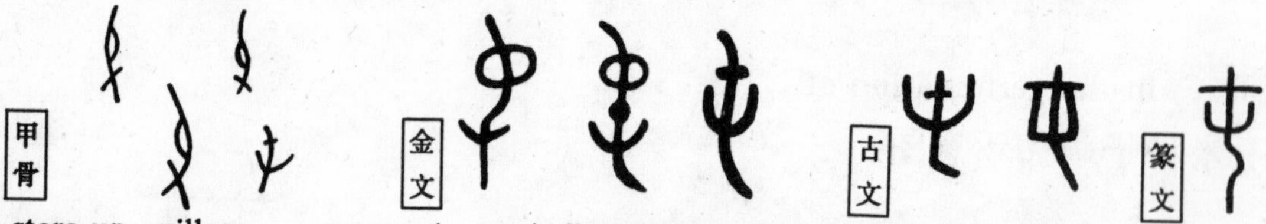

— to store up; village

囤，饨 tún；纯，莼 chún；噸＝吨 dūn；盹 dǔn；沌，炖，囤，钝，顿 dùn；肫，窀 zhūn.

* A flower in the bud. PLC.

象待放之花苞与叶形。

chūn

春

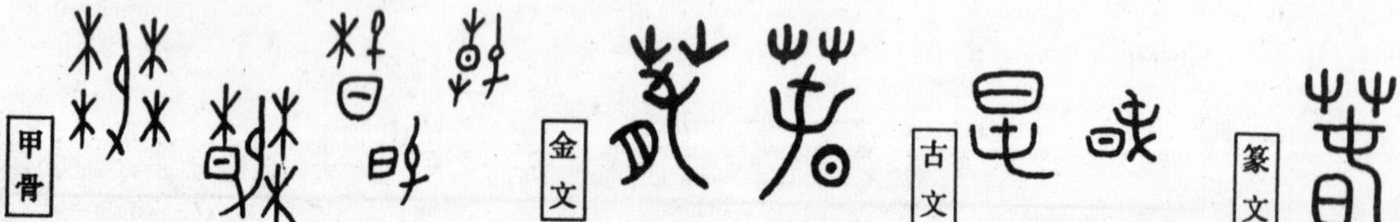

— spring; life vitality; love, lust, stirrings of love

椿 chūn；蠢 chǔn.

* A combination of 林 **lín**: forest or 草 **cǎo**: grass, 屯 **tún**: bud and 日 **rì**: the sun. 屯 **tún** was also a phonetic element. Later, the elements 屯 **tún** and 林 **lín** were merged together.

春字为林(草)，日，屯的组合。屯也是声符。

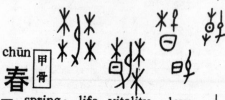

huá 華＝华 金文 古文 篆文

— flourishing, prosperous; brilliant

＃ 哗, 骅 huá; 哗 huā; 桦 huà.

* A flower with an upper plant-radical. [草 cǎo]

象花形。

---

róng 榮＝荣 金文 篆文

— to grow luxuriantly; to flourish; glory, honor; a surname

＃ 嵘, 蝾 róng; 劳 láo; 莺 yīng; 营, 茔, 荧, 莹, 萤, 萦, 滢 yíng.

* A bouquet, consisting of two flowers. The bottom element, 木 mù: tree, is a later addition.

象花木形。

---

píng 平 金文 古文 篆文

— flat, level; calm; impartial; to level

＃ 评, 枰, 鲆, 坪, (苹＝蘋) píng; 抨, 怦, 砰 pēng; 秤 chèng.

* Drawing of floating duckweed. PLC, 萍 píng: duckweed.

象浮萍形。

---

má 麻 金文 古文 篆文

— hemp, flax; pockmarks; benumbed, having a tingling feeling; a surname

＃ 嘛 ma; 摩 mó; 麾 huī; 糜, 縻, 靡, 蘼 mí; 靡 mǐ; 磨, 摩, 蘑, 魔 mó; 磨 mò.

* Drawing of two hemp plants (*Cannabis sativa*), used for their tough phloem fiber. Perhaps 广 guǎng: pictograph of a shed, implies storing hemp in a shed after harvest. [广 guǎng, 林 lín, 散 sǎn]

广下(剥)麻形。

43

guā
瓜
— melon
呱，胍 guā；呱，孤 gū；狐，弧 hú.

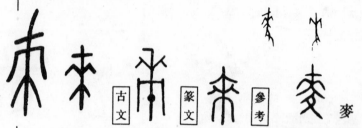

* A melon or gourd on the vine.
蔓上结瓜形。

lái
來＝来
— to come
莱，崃，徕，涞，铼 lái；睐，赉 lài.

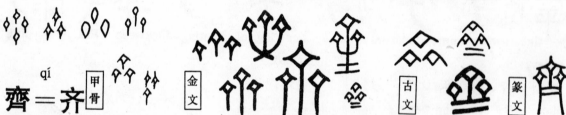

* A ripe wheat plant. PLC, 麥＝麦 mài；wheat; with an element denoting a footprint. Early Chinese pronunciation of the sounds "L" and "M" was very similar；since "来" is simpler and "come" is an everyday verb, therefore, 来 lái and 麦 mài were exchanged. Actually, wheat and barley originated in West Asia.   [止 zhǐ]

象一株成熟的麦形。上古来麦互借是由于当时发音中 L 与 M 不分和常用来字的缘故。

qí
齊＝齐
— neat, uniform; on a level with; simultaneously; all ready; similar; a surname
荠，脐 qí；跻，齑 jī；济，挤 jǐ；剂，济，鲚，荠，霁 jì；齋＝斋 zhāi.

* Wheat in the ear, or the wheat grains in a spike. PLC.

象小麦吐穗整齐之形。

hé
禾

— rice; standing grain, cereal

\# 和 hé, hè, huó, huò, hú；香 xiāng.

* A ripe rice plant. It is a radical for cereal plants.

象成熟的稻谷之形。

mǐ 米 [甲骨]

[篆文]

— rice; shelled or husked seed; metre

\# 籹，胈，眯 mǐ；咪，眯 mī；迷，谜，醚，糜，麋 mí；氣＝气 qì；屎 shǐ；粥 zhōu：gruel, porridge.

* An attempt to draw grains of rice. The "十" may be a mnemonic symbol.

象米粒形。

guǒ 果 [甲骨]

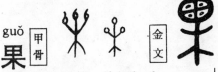 [金文]

 [篆文]

— fruit; result; if indeed

\# 蜾，裹 guǒ；踝 huái；棵，窠，稞，颗，髁 kē；课 kè；裸 luǒ.

* A tree bearing fruit.　[木 mù]

树上结果之形。

cì 朿 [甲骨]

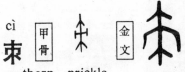 [金文] [篆文]

— thorn, prickle

\# 刺 cì：splinter, to stab；棗＝枣 zǎo：jujube, Chinese date；棘 jí：thorn bushes; brambles.

* A plant with thorns or prickles.　[木 mù]

象有芒刺的植物。

lì 栗 [甲骨]

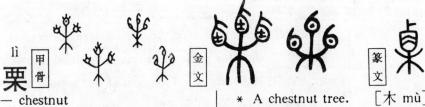 [金文] [篆文]

— chestnut

\# 傈，溧，篥 lì.

* A chestnut tree.　[木 mù]

象栗树形

mǒu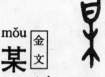

某 金文 古文 篆文

— certain, some

谋 móu；媒，煤 méi.

* A combination of 甘 **gān**：sweet and 木 **mù**：tree；the character may indicate a kind of fruit, 梅 **méi**：plum. PLC.　　[甘 **gān**, 木 **mù**]

某从甘(古文从口)从木，表示酸果。

zhú

竹 金文 篆文

— bamboo

* Two bamboo branches with leaves. 竹 **zhú** is an upper radical.　　[个 **gè**：drawing of a bamboo]

竹枝叶并立形。

2.3　Fauna　动物

2.3.1—Aquatic Animals, Reptiles and Insects　水生动物,爬行动物和昆虫

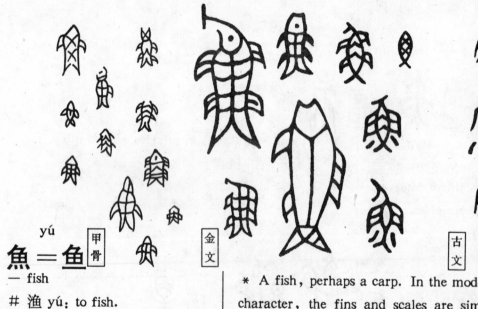

yú

魚＝鱼 甲骨 金文 古文 篆文

— fish

渔 yú：to fish.

* A fish, perhaps a carp. In the modern form of this character, the fins and scales are simplified into the element 田 **tián**, and the four dots at the bottom derive from the tail fin.　　[龟 **guī**, 燕 **yàn**]

鱼的侧视图。

bǐng
丙 甲骨 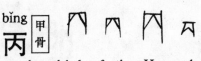 金文 古文 篆文

— the third of the Heavenly stems; third

柄，炳 bǐng；病 bìng.

* The tail fin of a fish. PLC.
象鱼尾之形。

bèi
貝＝贝 甲骨  金文 古文 篆文

— shellfish; cypraea, cowry; a surname

狈，钡 bèi；坝 bà；败 bài.

* The ventral view of a cowry shell. Cowry shells were used as money in the early stages of civilization; thus, this pictogram is a radical referring to money, property or treasure.
宝贝的腹视图。

guī
龜＝龟 甲骨 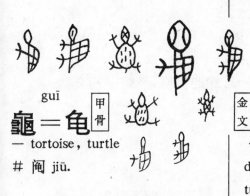 金文 古文 篆文

— tortoise, turtle

阄 jiū.

* The side view of a turtle. The simplified character is derived from the ancient simplified writing of the word turtle.
龟的侧视图。

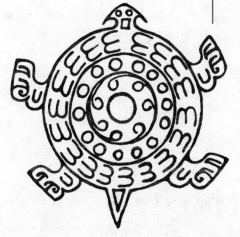

▲ Detail from the inside of a bronze vessel, a turtle motif (*after Jessica Rawson*).
青铜器铭纹・龟。

▲ A clay vessel with a fish motif. Banpo, the Neolithic.
半坡彩陶盆・鱼。仰韶文化。

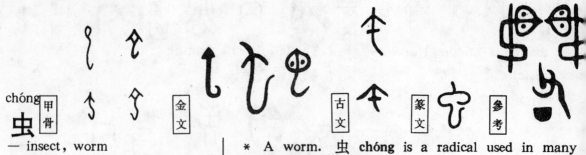

chóng 虫 甲骨 金文

— insect, worm

融 róng.

* A worm. 虫 **chóng** is a radical used in many characters meaning for worm or insect.

象虫形。

tā 它 甲骨 金文 古文 篆文

— it

铊 tā; 舵 duò; 蛇 shé, yí.

* A cobra-like snake. PLC, 蛇 **shé**：snake, serpent. [虫 chóng]

"它"字刻画一条蛇的轮廓,是蛇字初文。

yě 也 金文 篆文

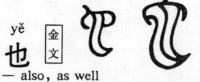

— also, as well

池,弛,驰 chí; 地 de, dì; 他,她 tā; 迤 yí, yǐ.

* Derived from 它 **tā**, meaning snake. PLC. [虫 chóng, 它 tā]

"也"字被认为是由它字发展而来。

měng 黽＝黾 甲骨 古文 篆文

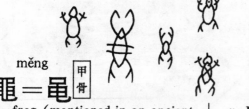

— frog (mentioned in an ancient book)

黾 miǎn, mǐn; 绳 shéng; 蝇 yíng; 鼍 tuó：Chinese alligator; 鼋 yuán：soft-shelled turtle.

* May be a drawing of a frog. 黽 **měng** is a radical for certain reptiles. [龟 guī]

在古书里,黽指一种蛙。

lóng
龍＝龙 甲骨
— dragon

＃ 茏，咙，泷，珑，栊，胧，
砻，聋，笼 lóng；陇，垄，拢，
笼 lǒng；宠 chǒng；庞 páng；袭
xí.

* The dragon is a frequently used symbol in China. It is a remnant of ancient tribal totems. The original form of the dragon may have been a snake used as a totem by a powerful clan. This clan conquered weaker clans whose totems were deer, tigers or even fish. The dragon, which bore many features of these other creatures, eventually appeared as a new unified emblem for the new and larger clan or nation. The dragon in China indicates an emperor, the *yang*, or even a bridegroom.

象中国龙形。

wàn
萬＝万 甲骨 金文
— ten thousand; myriad;
absolutely; a surname

＃ 趸 dǔn；厉，疠，励，砺，
粝，蛎 lì；迈 mài.

* A scorpion with pincers, a segmented body and curved tail tipped with a venomous sting. Later, the pincers were simplified into a grass-radical. The stroke on the tail indicates a numeric value and the lower surrounding strokes may be a form of the hand element (cf. 离 lí). 万 **wàn** is a peculiarly Chinese number unit, which also appears in the American Indian languages. [十 shí，百 bǎi，千 qiān]

象蝎之形。全世界只有中国人和印第安人以万做
为数的单位之一。对史前人来说，能数到万确实象
蝎子那样可怕。

49

2.3.2—Mammals 哺乳动物

zhì

豸

— an insect without feet or legs
(mentioned in ancient book)

* A wild beast with an open mouth, fangs, legs, and a tail. Its relation to the insect described in the ancient book is unclear. It is a radical in some characters referring to beasts. 〔肉 ròu〕

象野兽形。

bào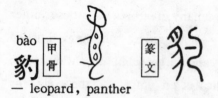

豹

— leopard, panther

* A leopard with its spots shown. The right-hand part 勺 **sháo** derives from the outline of a leopard's back and its spot (a dot). See above.

象身上有花斑点的豹形。

néng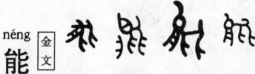

能

— can, ability

\# 熊 xióng.

* A bear. The two claws are placed on the right side in the vertical positioning. Compare the mouth and fangs in this character with those in 豸 **zhì** and 鼠 **shǔ**. PLC, 熊 **xióng**: bear, raging (flames); with a lower fire-radical. 熊 **xióng** is derived from "roasting a bear". 〔肉 ròu, 龙 lóng, 火 huǒ〕

象张口行走的熊形。

shǔ

鼠

— mouse

\# 竄 ＝ 窜 cuàn: to flee; 撺, 蹿, 镩 cuān.

* A mouse with an upturned mouth and teeth, and a long tail.

象牙齿发达的老鼠形。

hǔ 虎 〔甲骨〕〔金文〕〔古文〕〔篆文〕

— tiger

＃ 唬，琥 hǔ；彪 biāo.

* A hunter or soldier wearing a headdress made of a tiger's head. The picture-writing of "tiger's head" is a common phonetic element as well as a radical meaning "tiger". [虍 hū，蒙 méng]

甲骨文中有象虎形之字，后借用戴虎头头饰的人形为虎字，参见蒙等字。

lù 鹿 〔甲骨〕〔金文〕〔古文〕〔篆文〕

— deer

＃ 漉，辘，麓 lù；麠 áo；镳 biāo；塵＝尘 chén；麇 mí；麇 qún.

* This character consists of two components—the upper part is the deer's eye and antlers；the lower part，比 bǐ，represents the deer's legs.

象鹿形。

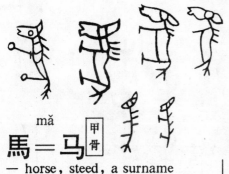

mǎ 馬＝马 〔甲骨〕〔金文〕〔古文〕〔篆文〕

— horse, steed, a surname

＃ 码，玛，犸，蚂 mǎ；吗 má，mǎ，ma；蚂，妈 mā；骂，蚂 mà；闯 chuǎng；笃 dǔ.

* The upper part of 马 mǎ represants the horse's eye and mane, and the lower part its legs and tail.

象马形。

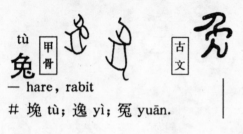 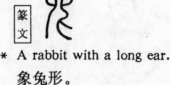

tù
兔
— hare, rabit
塊 tù；逸 yì；冤 yuān.

* A rabbit with a long ear.
象兔形。

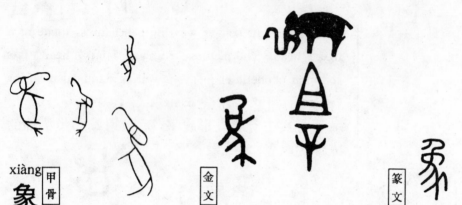

xiàng
象
— elephant; to image; to resemble, seem, like
像，橡 xiàng.

* An elephant with its tusks, trunk and ears shown (comp. 兔 tù and 豕 shǐ). In prehistoric times, there were a lot of elephants in northern China, but they disappeared gradually. When one person had seen the rare beast, he might then have given a glowing account of his adventure to his friends, who could only have **imagined** the animal.

象大象形。

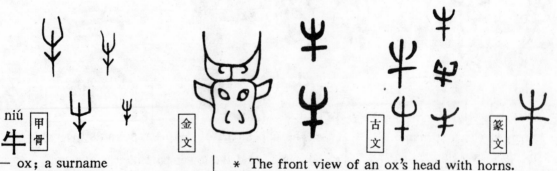

niú
牛
— ox; a surname
件 jiàn；牢 láo.

* The front view of an ox's head with horns.
［牢 láo］
牛的头部前视形。

yáng
羊 甲骨 金文
— sheep

\# 佯，洋，徉，烊 yáng；養＝养，氧，癢＝痒 yǎng；恙，樣＝样 yàng；咩 miē：baa，bleat；鲜 xiān，xiǎn；庠，祥，翔，详 xiáng.

* Drawing of the long face, beard and horns of a ram.   〔鲜 xiān，羞 xiū，羌 qiāng〕

羊字源于对羊双角和长脸的刻划。

古文 篆文

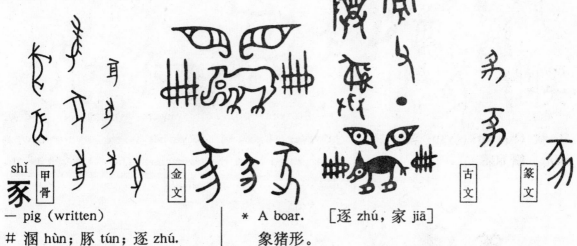

shǐ
豕 甲骨 金文
— pig (written)

\# 溷 hùn；豚 tún；逐 zhú.

* A boar.   〔逐 zhú，家 jiā〕

象猪形。

古文 篆文

▶ A pig-shaped clay kettle. Excavated at Dawenkou, the Neolithic. High 21.6 cm.

夹沙红陶兽形器·猪。大汶口出土。

hài 亥 甲骨 金文 古文 篆文

— the last of the twelve Earthly Branches.

氦，骇 hài；咳 hāi；孩，骸 hái；该，赅 gāi；劾，阂，核 hé；核 hú；颏 kē；咳 ké；刻 kè.

* Supposedly a cognate of 豕 shǐ：pig, which was borrowed to be used for one of the twelve Earthly Branches.

亥为豕的变形。

▶ Rubbing of a pig motif from a Neolithic clay vessel, Hemudu culture.

黑陶猪纹方钵拓片。河姆渡文化。

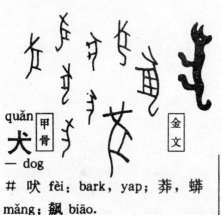

quǎn 犬 甲骨 金文 古文 篆文

— dog

吠 fèi：bark, yap；莽，蟒 mǎng；飙 biāo.

* Derived from the picture writing of a dog; however, traces of the earlier image have somewhat disappeared from the character. The dot might be the dog's tail.　[犭 as radical]

犬源于狗的象形文字。

xiān 鲜 金文 古文 篆文

— delicious；fresh

鲜，藓 xiǎn；癣 xuǎn.

* The combination of a fish and a ram.　[鱼 yú and 羊 yáng]

鱼和羊的组合，表示味道鲜美。

nüè 虐 金文 古文 篆文

— cruel; ill-treat

瘧＝疟 nüè；谑 xuè.

* Shows a tiger clawing. The lower part is the tiger's claw.　　［虎 hǔ，又 yòu：the action of hand, notice the direction of ″hand″］

虎用爪伤人,表示肆虐。

jiǎo

角 [甲骨] [金文] [古文] [篆文]

— horn; angle; corner; cape

角 jué；(确＝確 què).

* An ox horn. 角 jiǎo is also a radical.　　［解 jiě］

象牛角之形。

lì

麗＝丽 [甲骨] [金文] [篆文]

— beautiful

俪 lì；骊，鹂，丽，鹂 lí；逦 lǐ；灑＝洒 sǎ；酾，曬＝晒 shài；酾 shī.

* A deer with beautiful antlers, or possibly a giraffe. PLC.

象鹿有双角,表示美丽和匹配。

sì

兕 [甲骨]  [古文] [篆文]

— male rhinoceros (mentioned in ancient books)

* Picture writing of a rhino.

象犀牛形。

2.3.3—Birds 鸟类

niǎo

鳥 = 鸟 甲骨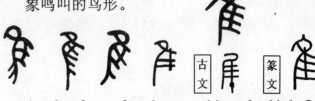

— bird

茑 niǎo; 鸣 míng: the cry of birds.

* A bird with a beak or bill; the lower four dots represent the talons and feathers.

象鸟形。

wū

烏 = 乌 金文

— crow, black.

呜, 钨 wū; 坞 wù.

* A crying bird. The traditional interpretation of this character's meaning is that the crow is too black for its eye to be seen.   [乌 niǎo]

象鸣叫的鸟形。

zhuī 甲骨

隹

— short-tailed bird

椎, 锥 zhuī; 椎 chuí; 崔, 催, 摧 cuī; 璀 cuǐ; 翟 dí, zhái; 堆 duī; 碓 duì; 淮 huái; 集 jí; 進 = 进 jìn; 谁 shéi, shuí; 售 shòu; 睢 suī; 隼, 槫 sǔn; 推 tuī; 维, 惟, 帷, 唯 wéi; 唯 wěi; 隻 = 只 zhī; 稚, 雉 zhì; 準 = 准 zhǔn; 雀 què, qiǎo.

* Another form of a picture writing of a bird. It is a common pictorial element, generally used in characters denoting birds and fowl.   [鸟 niǎo, 隹 jiā]

隹象鸟形。

yàn 甲骨
燕
— swallow
燕 yān.

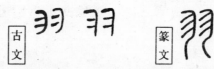篆文

* A flying swallow carrying a twig in its bill.
象飞燕衔枝形。

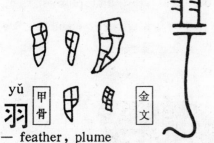

yǔ 甲骨 金文
羽
— feather, plume
翅 chì: wing, shark's fin;
扇, 煽 shān; 扇, 骟 shàn; 翔
xiáng; 栩, 诩 xǔ; 習 = 习 xí;
翊, 翌 yì.

古文 篆文 羽

* The ancient pictograph is a picture of a bird's wing. The modern 羽 **yǔ** comes from a drawing of two plumes.
象鸟羽形。

fēi 甲骨 金文
非
— un, non, etc.; wrong,
evildoing; no, not; simply must
扉, 蜚, 绯 fēi; 腓 féi; 诽,
菲 fěi; 痱 fèi.

古文 篆文

* Shows the flapping wings of a bird. PLC.
象鸟儿拍动的翅膀。

fēi
飛 = 飞
— to fly

篆文 参考

assemble 集 jí

* A flying bird. [升 shēng: to move upward]
飞鸟形。

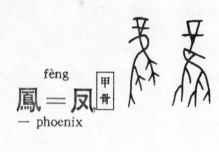

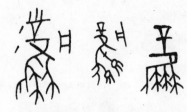

fèng

鳳＝凤 [甲骨]
— phoenix

* A bird with a beautiful crest and plumes. The surrounding element 凡 **fán** is a phonetic element. See below.   [凡 fán, 鸟 niáo, 风 fēng]
象头上有羽冠的鸟。

▶ Inscriptions on an oracle bone: *The phoenix stops (the wind falls).* (*After Kuo Mo-jo (2).*)
卜辞·凤止＝风止。

fēng

風＝风 [篆文]
— wind
♯ 枫，疯，砜 fēng；讽 fěng；
岚 lán；飒 sà.

* Derived from 鳳＝凤 **fèng**, with the lower 鸟 **niǎo**: bird, replaced by 虫 **chóng**: worm. PLC.
[凤 fèng]
风源于凤，假借。

zào

喿 [金文] [古文] [篆文]
— chirp of birds
♯ 操 cāo；缲，臊 sào；臊 sāo；
澡，藻 zǎo；噪，燥，躁 zào.

* Three "mouths" on the tree imply the songs of birds.   [口 kǒu, 木 mù]
树上的鸟鸣声。

huán

萑 甲骨 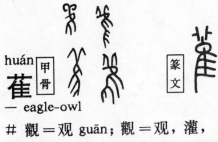 篆文

— eagle-owl

\# 觀＝观 guān；觀＝观，灌，罐，鸛 guàn；歡＝欢，獾 huān；權＝权，顴 quán；勸＝劝 quàn；護＝护 hù；獲＝获，鑊，蠖 huò；劐 huō；舊＝旧 jiù.

 参考

* An eagle-owl (great horned owl).　[隹 zhuī，鸛 guàn：stork.]

象长耳猫头鹰。

huò

霍 甲骨 

— suddenly; quickly

\# 霍 huò；攉 huō.

 金文　　篆文

* Shows birds flying quickly in the rain.　[雨 yǔ，隹 zhuī]

象雨中疾飞的鸟儿。

cháo

巢 甲骨　金文　篆文

— nest

\# 剿 cháo，jiǎo；繅 sāo.

* A bird's nest in a tree.　[木 mù]

树上鸟窝。

xī

西 甲骨　金文　 古文　篆文

— west

\# （牺＝犧），硒，茜 xī；栖 qī；茜 qiàn.

* A bird's nest. PLC.　[巢 cháo]

鸟巢形。

59

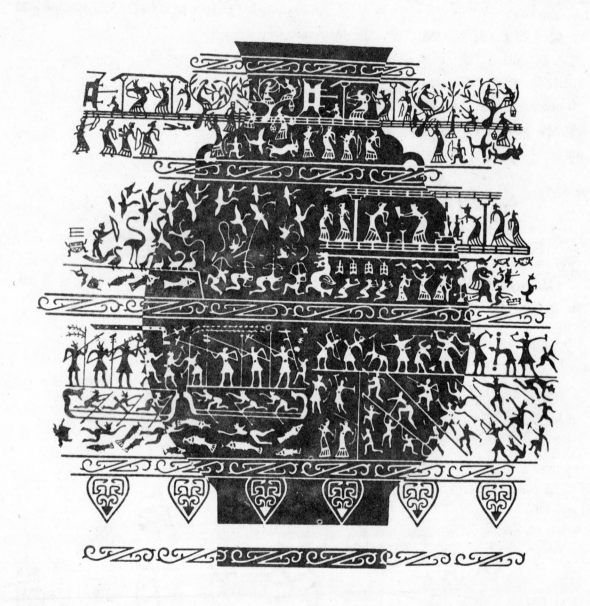

Design on a bronze wine jar, Warring States Period.

战国铜器图案。

Chapter 3

HUNTING AND AGRICULTURE 狩猎与农耕

Progress from a hunting and gathering way of life to the domestication of plants and animals is called the Food-Producing Revolution. This occured during the Neolithic period. Great improvements in the manufacture of stone implements are associated with this change. In this chapter, the entries will show us a panoramic view of the struggle of early Chinese to survive.

从采集渔猎靠天吃饭,到发明农业和畜牧业控制食物的生产过程是人类经济生活中的一次大跃进,这一跃进被考古学家们称之为新石器时代革命。这一章中的汉字将向读者展现一幅三千多年前中国人为生存而斗争的生动的全景画。

Hunting and harvesting. Rubbing of a brick from a tomb. Sichuan Province, Han Dynasty.

汉代画象砖·弋射收获图。成都杨子山出土,46cm×42cm。

3.1   Hunting   狩猎

Five bowmen. Rock painting of Levant, Spain, the Stone Age.

五个弓手。西班牙列文特岩画,石器时代(自《世界美术史》第一卷,109页)。

3.1.1—Animal's Footprint   蹯

biàn 采

— archaic form of 辨 biàn: to distinguish, differentiate
#悉: to be familiar with, 蟋 xī;
释 shì: to explain.

* The footprint of an animal. See below. [采 cǎi]

For prehistoric people, the discovery and recognition of animal prints was important for both hunting and avoiding the dangers of prowling beasts. If a hunter found an animal's footprint with which he was **familiar**, he could **explain** to his son or partner what kind of animal was nearby. The assistant would **look carefully** at the footprint, and could learn the skills of tracking.

动物足印形。古辨字,与“采”字易混,后废弃不用。

对史前先民来说,在打猎中发现和识别动物的足印是十分重要的。当一个猎人发现一种他所熟**悉**的动物足印,他可以向他的儿子或助手解**释**周围有何种动物,并决定追猎或逃避;而晚辈则会将这种足印仔细**审**视一**番**,从中学到打猎的技巧。

fān

番

金文

— a course, a turn; aboringines
幡，翻，蕃 fān；蕃，蹯 fán；
播 bō；潘 pān；蟠 pán.

古文　篆文

* A combination of an animal's footprint and a
symbal of hunting：田 tián. (See also 留 liú and 畜
chù). PLC，蹯 fán：animal's footprint；with a foot-
radical：足 zú. [采 biàn，田 tián]

动物足印和"田"的组合,这里"田"可理解为一个
表示狩猎的符号。

shěn

審＝审

金文

— to look closely at
婶，瀋＝沈 shěn.

古文　篆文

* May depict a hunter (legs shown) standing over and
examining an animal's footprint.　　[大 dà，番 fān，
六 liù, and 申 shēn]

"审"可理解为一个猎人弯腰审视胯下的动物足
印,宝盖头象胯下形,见大字。

◀ Some footprints of carnivorous animals.

几种肉食动物的足印。

1. badger　2. wolf　3. tiger　4. bear

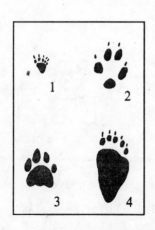

▶ Some footprints of hoofed animals (mostly
herbivorous).

马类和几种常见偶蹄类动物的足印。

1. wild ox　2. antelope　3. ram　4. deer
　5. wild boar　6. horse　7. ass

(采自尤玉柱：《乌兰察布岩画中的动物》,
《乌兰察布岩画》,326 页。)

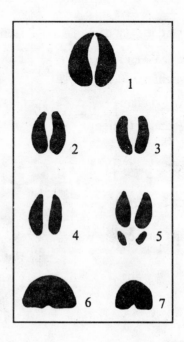

3. 1. 2—Tools for Hunting 打猎工具

yā

— branch or fork (of a tree)

* Pictograph.
象树杈枝丫。

gàn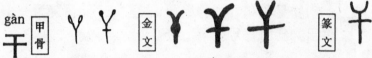

— to do; to fight; trunk
干：to offend，矸，肝竿酐
gān；杆，秆，赶，撵 gǎn；幹，
幹＝干，肝 gàn；岸 àn；犴
hān；旱，汗，捍，悍，焊 hàn；
奸，歼 jiān；刊 kān；轩 xuān；
讦 jié.

* The dot (later a horizontal stroke) indicates the stem
of a tree branch. Branches were used as perhistoric
weapons for both hunting and war. [丫 yā，单 dān]
用一点（后发展为一横画）指示树杈的枝干。枝干
作为原始工具，用于打猎和战争。

dān
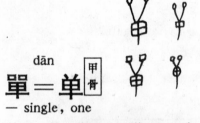
單＝单

— single, one
殫，箪，郸 dān；掸 dǎn；瘅，
惮，弹 dàn；婵，禅，蝉，单（单
于）chán；阐 chǎn；单（姓），掸
（族），禅（让）shàn；蕲，弹
tán；戰＝战 zhàn：to fight.

* A prehistoric weapon made from a tree branch with
stone knives and a net (or shield) attached to it. PLC.
[战 zhàn：to fight，戈 gē，and see above]
系有石刀的树杈，中间可能表示网或盾牌。

wǎng
网

— simplified from of 網 wǎng：
net.
罔，辋，惘，魍 wǎng.

* A net. As an upper radical, the form of 网 **wǎng** is
flattened to become "⺲". [罔 wǎng：deceive,
cheat；亡 wáng]
象网形，网是一个返朴归真的好简化字。

▶ A boat-shaped clay kettle with a net motif. Excavated at Beishouling, the Neolithic.

船形陶壶·网。北首岭遗址出土 (4840—4170 BC)。

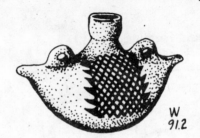

W 91.2

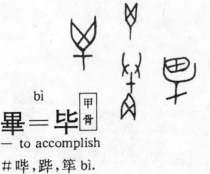

bì 甲骨

畢＝毕

— to accomplish

哔, 跸, 筚 bì.

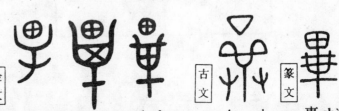

金文   古文   篆文

* An ancient net made from a tree branch, see 事 shì and 禽 qín. The upper part 田 tián is a symbol of hunting.　[单 dān]

象一种用树枝做的网。"田"为一个表示狩猎的符号。

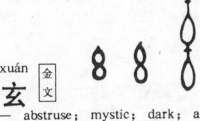

xuán 金文

玄

— abstruse; mystic; dark; a surname

痃 xuán; 泫, 眩, 炫 xuàn; 弦, 舷 xián; 牽＝牵 qiān.

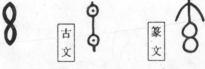

古文   篆文

* Bolas——an ancient throwing-weapon made with two stones fastened to the ends of a rope, see 畜 chù. PLC.

绳球象形。绳球为一种在长绳或皮条两端系有石块的狩猎工具,用来投向猎物(如鹿),以缠绕猎物的腿等处。

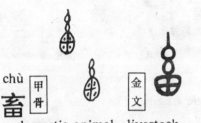

chù 甲骨

畜

— domestic animal, livestock

搐 chù; 蓄 xù: to store up, to harbour.

金文   篆文

* A combination of 玄 xuán: bolas, and 田 tián: a symbol of hunting.

绳球(玄)与田的组合。

3. 1. 3—Fishing and Hunting   渔猎

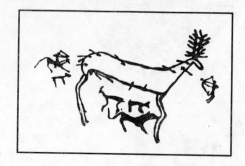

◀ **Rock painting** • **Hunting.** (*After Gai, S. L.* (2) *fig.* 129.)

岩画•射猎。

gǔn

鲧 甲骨 金文 古文 篆文 参考

— name of a legendary ancestor.

* A hand fishing with a line.   [鱼 yú, 系 xì or 系 mì, 玄 xuán]

钓鱼之形。鲧是夏禹父亲的名字,传说中最早开始建造城市的人。

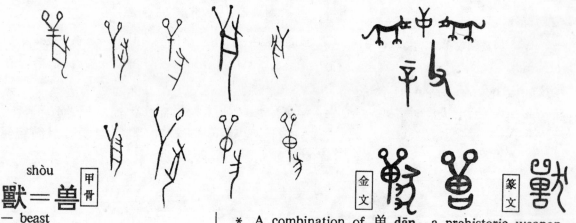

shòu

獸＝兽 甲骨 金文 篆文

— beast

* A combination of 单 dān：a prehistoric weapon, and 犬 quǎn：dog. 兽 shòu：beast, and 狩 shòu：hunting, had the same origin. The modern character 狩 shòu is a pictophone.   [单 dān, 犬 quǎn]

用狩猎工具"干(单)"和犬表示打猎。古文兽狩一字。

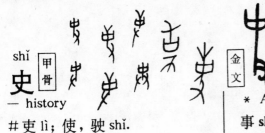

shǐ 甲骨

史
— history

吏 lì；使，驶 shǐ.

* A hand holding a hunting weapon. 史 shǐ：history,
事 shì：affair, 吏 lì：official, and 使 shǐ：to use, are
cognate characters. See below.

史象手持叉网形。史，吏，事，使四字同源。

shì 甲骨

事
— affair, matter；event,
accident；to do

* Depicts catching a boar with a branch-net. The
"boar" is simplified into a single stroke "一" in the
modern character 事 shì.　[单 dān，毕 bì，又 yòu,
史 shǐ]

用叉网捕捉野猪。

◀ Catching a boar with a branch-net
(after Kang, Yen. (3) p. 255).
用叉网捕获野猪。

zhuō 甲骨

卓
— outstanding

桌 zhuō；绰 chuō；绰 chuò；
悼 dào；掉 diào；淖 nào；棹，罩
zhào.

* A man with a net. The upper part is supposed to be
the simplified form of a bird. PLC, 罩 zhào：to cover；
topped a net-radical. [毕＝毕 bì，网 wǎng]

象叉网罩物形。

67

qín

离 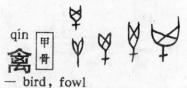 甲骨

— bird, fowl

檎，擒，噙 qín.

 金文　 古文　篆文

* A hand holding a net. Compare the hand and net with 事 shì. The upper 今 jīn is a phonetic element, thus, 禽 qín is a pictophone. It is also a PLC, 擒 qín: catch, with a hand-radical. See below.

手拿捕鸟网形，今声，擒本字。

lí

離＝离 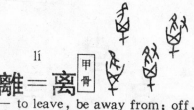 甲骨

— to leave, be away from; off, away, from; without, independent of

篱，漓，璃，缡 lí；魑 chī.

 古文　篆文

* Shows a bird being taken from a net. See above. [隹 zhuī, 禽 qín]

用手取出网内的鸟儿，可能是指鸟儿离开了伙伴。简化字中鸟儿彻底离开了。

zhī

隻＝只  甲骨

— measure-word, a piece of indeterminate character, which can usually be grabbed by hand; along

枳，咫 zhǐ；（織＝织 zhī；职 zhí；炽 chì；识，帜 zhì；识 shí).

金文　古文　篆文

* A hand grasping a bird. PLC. a pair, 萑 huán, 隹 zhuī, 又 yòu]

[雙＝双 shuāng:

象手抓获一只鸟儿形。

zhú

逐 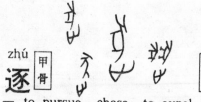 甲骨

— to pursue, chase; to expel; one by one, progressively

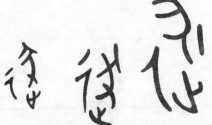 金文　篆文

* A combination of a boar and a footprint. It represents hunters chasing or driving a boar.

[豕 shǐ, 止 zhǐ, and 辶 chuò]

猎人追逐驱赶野猪。

duì

隊＝队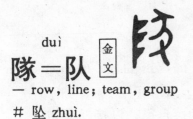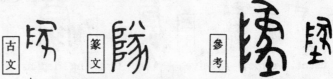

— row, line; team, group

坠 zhuì.

* A boar being driven over a cliff, just like the scene in the oil painting *Buffalos Jump*. PLC, 墜＝坠 zhuì: to fall; here 土 tǔ: soil, indicates the bottom of the cliff.　[阜 fù, 豕 shǐ]

队表示驱赶野猪坠下山崖。

tuàn

彖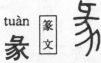

— a proper noun used in *The Book of Changes*（《易经》）

掾 yuàn；缘，椽 yuán；椽 chuán.

* Drawing of a dead boar. PLC.　[豕 shǐ]

彖死野猪形。

xiàn

臽

— pit (archaic)

谄 chǎn: to flatter；馅: filling, stuffing，陷: to sink, get stuck　xiàn；阎 yán；焰 yàn；掐 qiā: to pinch.

* A man setting a trap. The dirt clods and pitfall were replaced with the element 臼 jiù: mortar.　[人 rén, 臼 jiù]

人挖陷井之形。古文字中是指陷埋人牲以祭。

lì

隶

— under the jurisdiction; a person in servitude

逮 dǎi；棣 dì；隸＝隶 lì.

* A hand seizing an animal's tail. PLC, 逮 dǎi: to capture；逮 dài: to arrest, reach.　[又 yòu, 辶 chuò]

抓住猎物的尾巴。

69

mēng 蒙 甲骨 金文 篆文

— to cheat, dupe, deceive; unconscious

檬，朦，艨，蒙：to cover méng；蒙 měng：the Mongol nationality.

* Drawing depicts hunters disguising themselves in animal skins.　［冒 mào，豕 shǐ］

猎人用动物的毛皮伪装自己。以接近猎物。

qiāng 羌 甲骨 金文 古文 篆文

— an ancient nationality in China, the Qiang nationality, living in Sichuan Province

* A man with a ram headdress.　［羊 yáng，人 rén］

头戴羊角的人形。羌族是中国古代较大的民族。

jiāng 姜 甲骨 金文 古文 篆文

— a surname

* A woman with a ram headdress. ［羊 yáng，女 nǚ］

头戴羊角的女人形。姜为羌族女子之称。也是羌族、羌姓之称。

Bushman's rock painting · Hunter disguised in an ostrich skin.
伪装成鸵鸟的猎人正在接近猎物（自《世界美术史》第一卷 296）。

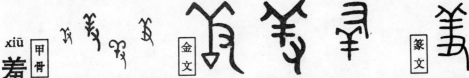

xiū 羞 甲骨 金文 篆文

— shy, bashful; shame; to feel ashamed

馐 xiū: dainty.

* A hand catching a ram. 丑 **chǒu** derives from 又 **yòu**: action of the hand. PLC. 〔羊 yáng, 丑 chǒu or 又 yòu〕

羞象手抓羊形,有进献和美味的意思。

zhì 雉 甲骨

— pheasant

古文 篆文

* To shoot an arrow at a bird. 矢 **shǐ** is also a phonetic element. 〔矢 shǐ, 隹 zhuī〕

象箭射鸟形。

Shooting · Rubbing of bricks from tombs. Han Dynasty.

汉代画像砖·射猎。

zhì 彘 甲骨

— boar

金文 篆文

* To shoot an arrow at a boar. 矢 **shǐ**: arrow, is also a phonetic element. 比 **bǐ** is a drawing of the boar's claws. 〔彖 tuàn, 矢 shǐ, 雉 zhì, 能 néng and 鹿 lù〕

象箭射中野猎形。

3.2   Agriculture   农业

At different times and in numerous places, many plants and animals have been domesticated. China is one of the original centers of agriculture, and dependence on millet and rice is characteristic of Chinese Neolithic agriculture. It has been suggested on somewhat speculative grounds that foxtail millet (*Setaria italica*) was cultivated before 6000 BC in the Yellow River basin and the loess highland of northern China. By 5000 BC rice (*Oryza sativa*) had probably been domesticated. This took place around the drainage area of the Yangtze River and the south eastern coast of China. Wheat and barley were introduced to China before 1300 BC, and the soy bean, perhaps around 1100 BC.

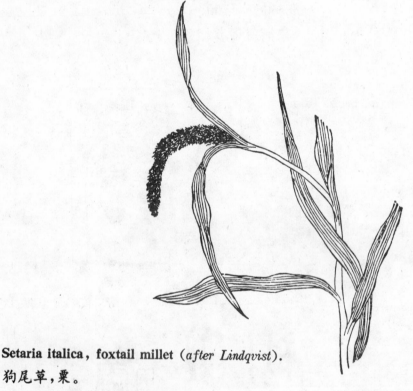

Setaria italica, foxtail millet (*after Lindqvist*).

狗尾草，粟。

中国是世界上农业起源中心之一，早在七、八千年以前就已进入相当繁荣的农耕阶段。中国考古发现的大量谷物遗存中，可以以粟(包括黍)和稻为代表。黄河流域广泛种植的粟，俗称小米，一般认为是由中国人首先从狗尾草驯化而来的。长江流域和东南沿海一带则在七千年以前，已经开始栽培稻谷，这在世界范围内属于最早的。伴随着农业的产生和发展，人类的定居生活也就更加稳固，往往形成大规模的聚落，为城市和国家的出现打下了基础。

3.2.5　Farmer's Tools　农具

"Slash-and-burn" may have been a principal feature of prehistoric farming. Chinese prehistoric farming implements were mainly made from stone, wood, bone and clam-shell. Bronze was an important material for making sacrificial utensils and weapons, not common farmer's tools.

中国原始的农具主要是用石、木、骨、蚌壳等物制成的,就是到了青铜时代,这种状况也没有很大的改善。因为青铜在古代中国有更重要的用途——祭祀与战争,只是到了铁器时代,大规模的毁林种田才得以实现。

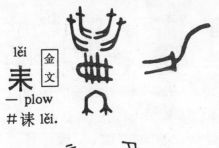 

lěi 金文
耒
— plow
诔 lěi.

* An ancient plow. This element is used mainly as a radical in characters referring to farming.

一种下面带有两个叉的木制翻土农具。

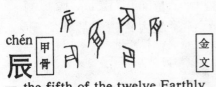 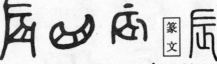

chén 甲骨 金文 篆文
辰
— the fifth of the twelve Earthly Branches; celestial bodies; time
宸, 晨 chén；唇 chún；娠 shēn；蜃 shèn；振, 赈, 震 zhèn.

* An ancient farmer's sickle made of clam-shell. PLC, 蜃 shèn：clam；with a lower worm-radical. 辰 chén is used in certain characters as an element that means "to move."　[农 nóng, 蓐 rù]

商代以蚌壳为镰,在蚌壳上穿二孔并用绳索缚于拇指,用以掐断禾穗。以辰为部件的汉字多有"动"意。

3.2.2—Farming　农耕

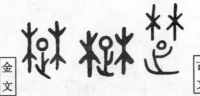

chǔ 甲骨 金文 古文 篆文
楚
— name of ancient kingdom, roughly equivalent to modern Hubei Province; pang, suffering; clear, neat; a surname
礎＝础 chǔ；憷 chù.

* The combination of 林 lín：forest, and 疋 pǐ：another form of 足 zú：foot. 楚 chǔ shows man marching into the forest. 足 zú is also a phonetic element.　[正 zhèng]

楚字上为林下为足,表示拔除荆棘,征服森林。

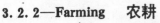

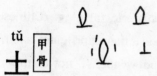

tǔ 甲骨
土
— soil, earth; land; native
吐，钍 tǔ；吐 tù；肚 dù；杜 dù；社 shè：the god of the land.

* A dirt clod in a field. The upper cross represents the clod. ［士 shì］

象地面上的土块之形。

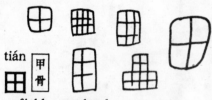
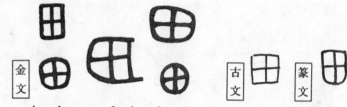

tián 甲骨
田
— field, cropland; a surname
畋：to hunt，佃，钿 tián；佃，甸，钿 diàn；男 nán；亩 mǔ；界 jiè.

* A picture of the farmland with low earthen embankments between fields. It is also a symbol for hunting. (See also 番 fān, 畜 chù, 雷 léi.)

象农田分割之形。一说象古代田猎战阵之形。

jiāng 甲骨
疆 金文
— border; territory
僵，缰 jiāng.

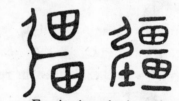

* Emphasizes the boundary ridges between fields. The bow, 弓 gōng, was used for measurement; 土 tǔ: land, is a meaning element ［田 tián，弓 gōng，土 tǔ］

疆字强调田地之间的界线，弓为丈量土地的工具，土为意符。

fǔ 甲骨
甫 金文
— just, only (written)
脯，辅 fǔ；逋 bū；補＝补，捕，哺 bǔ；铺 pū；匍，葡，莆，脯，蒲 pú；浦，埔，圃 pǔ；铺 pù.

* A single seedling in a field. Later, the "seedling" was replaced by a phonetic, 父 fù. PLC, 圃 pǔ: garden, plot. ［生 shēng，田 tián，父 fù］

甫即圃，象田地里生长的小苗。

74

miáo 苗 [篆文]

— seedling; something resembling a young plant

描，瞄 miáo；喵 miāo；猫 māo；锚 máo.

* Two seedlings (the grass-radical) in field.
[草 cǎo，田 tián]

象田地中小苗之形。

nóng 農＝农 [甲骨]

— agriculture; farmer

侬，哝，浓，脓 nóng.

* Hands holding a *chen*-sickle. The 囟 **xìn** was later added as a phonetic element. In the modern form of this character, both the hands and the ancient phonetic element were merged into the unit 曲 **qǔ**. [草 cǎo，辰 chén，又 yòu]

象手持辰镰从事农作之形。

rù 蓐 [甲骨]

— straw mat or mattress

辱 rǔ；溽，褥，缛 rù.

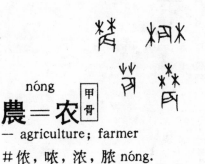

[篆文]

* A farmer's hand holding a *chen*-sickle to weed. PLC, 薅 **hāo**: to weed. [农 nóng，草 cǎo，辰 chén，寸 cùn and 耨 nòu: weeding hoe, weeding]

象手持辰镰除草之形，是薅的本字。

yì 藝＝艺 [甲骨]

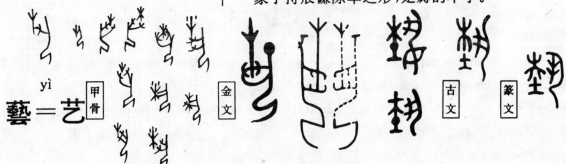

[金文] [古文] [篆文]

— skill, art

\# 呓 yì.

* A farmer planting a seedling. The character is topped with a grass-radical. The lower part of this character 云 **yún** perhaps originated as the farmer's foot and leg. The simplified form is a pictophone, see 乙 **yǐ.** [草 cǎo, 热 rè]

象人栽种植物之形。

fēng 丰 [甲骨]  [金文] [古文] 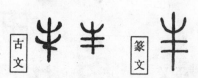 [篆文]

— abundant; great; fine-looking; a surname

\# 邦, 梆, 帮 bāng; 蚌 bàng; 峰, 烽, 蜂, 锋 fēng; 逢, 缝 féng; 缝 fèng; 蓬, 篷 péng.

* Packing the roots of a plant with soil. See below.

象用土包住植物根部之形。

fēng 封 [甲骨]  [金文] [古文] [篆文]

— to seal; to confer (a title, territory, etc.); feudalism.

\# 幫=帮 bāng.

* A hand planting a tree (cf. 艺 **yì**). The trees might have been planted to mark the boundary of a fief.

[丰 fēng, 木 mù, 土 tǔ, 又 yòu or 寸 cùn]

用手将树苗载入土中。

fèng 奉 [甲骨] 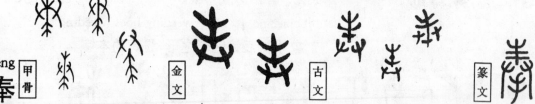 [金文] [古文] [篆文]

— to give or present with respect; receive; esteem, revere; wait upon, attend;

\# 俸 fèng: pay, salary; 捧 pěng: to extol, flatter; 棒 bàng.

* Two hands holding a plant. 丰 **fēng** is also a phonetic element. The lower 手 **shǒu**: hand, was added later as a radical. PLC, 捧 **pěng**: to hold in both hands. [丰 fēng, 又 yòu or 共 gòng, 手 shǒu]

双手持树苗形,奉也是形声字。

yǐ
以
金文  古文 篆文

— to use；to take；according to
；so as to
似，姒 sì；似 shì.

* A farmer using a spade or an ancient plow.
[厶 sī，人 rén，耜 sì：plow]
象人用耒耜(sì)形。以字中厶即耜。

shì
氏
甲骨 金文 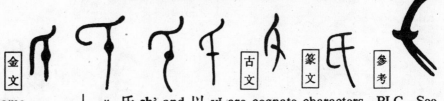 古文 篆文 参考

— family name, surname
舐 shì；祇 qí；纸，抵 zhǐ.

* 氏 shì and 以 yǐ are cognate characters. PLC. See above.
氏、以两字同源。

lì
利
甲骨 金文  古文 篆文

— shape；benefit；favourable
犁，梨，蜊，黎，藜，黧 lí；
俐，莉，痢，猁 lì.

* Ancient forms of 利 lì show land being plowed to prepare for planting rice. Dots represent the clods of dirt. However, the modern form of 利 lì is a combination of 禾 hé：rice and 刀 dāo：knife, actually implying the harvest.　[禾 hé，刀 dāo]
象以耒刺地种禾之形。古文字中的点象翻起的泥土。

jǐng
井
甲骨 金文 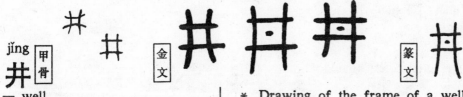 篆文

— well
阱 jǐng：trap；（讲＝講 jiǎng；进＝進 jìn.）

* Drawing of the frame of a well. The prehistoric oblong wells have been discovered in the Yellow River basin.
象井栏四木相交之形。中国人发明水井是在龙山文化早期(约公元前 2800 年)。有了水井,先民就可以摆脱河湖的地理限制了。

3. 2. 3—Harvest, Food Processing and Storage   农作物的收获加工与贮藏

cǎi
采
— to pick

彩，睬，踩，采 cǎi，菜，采 cài.

* A hand picking leaves.   [爪 zhǎo，木 mù]
用手摘采树叶。

bǐng
秉
— to hold (written)

* A hand grasping a rice plant.   [禾 hé，又 yòu]
手持一棵谷子(禾)。

jiān
兼
— to combine, merge; simultaneously, side by side; and
鹣 jiān；廉，簾＝帘，镰 lián；谦 qiān；歉 qiàn；嫌 xián；赚 zhuàn.

* A hand grasping two rice plants at the same time. [秉 bǐng]
手持两棵谷子。

lí
厘
— 1/1000, 1/100; a fraction
嫠 lí.

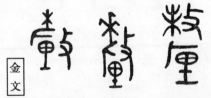

* The upper element indicates the threshing of wheat. 里 **lí** is a phonetic element.   [来 lái，父 fù]
对谷物或小麦进行脱粒。

wǔ 午 甲骨  金文 古文 篆文

— the seventh of the twelve Earthly Branches; noon

\# 仵，忤 wǔ；杵 chǔ；浒 hǔ；许，浒 xǔ.

* A wooden pestle. PLC, 杵 chǔ：pestle；with a wood-radical.

象木杵之形。

jiù 臼 古文 篆文

— mortar

\# 舅，舊＝旧 jiù.

* A cutaway view of a mortar.

象臼的剖视图。

yǎo 舀 篆文 参考

— to ladle out

\# 蹈 dǎo；稻 dào：rice；滔，韬 tāo.

* A hand filling a mortar with rice.　［爪 zhǎo，臼 jiù］

象用手从臼内取米形。

▶ Pounding rice.

杵臼图。（采自《中国科技史资料选编·农业机械》，257 页，原书采自徐光启《农政全书》。）

chōng

春 甲骨  金文  篆文

— to pound

樁 = 桩 zhuāng.

* A depiction of husking rice with a mortar and pestle.   [又 yòu, 午 wǔ, 臼 jiù, 秦 qín]

象双手持杵舂臼中米之形。

kāng

康 甲骨 金文 古文 篆文

— health; a surname

慷 kāng.

* Sifting flour from bran. PLC, 糠 kāng: chaff.

象筛糠皮之形。

qín

秦 甲骨  金文 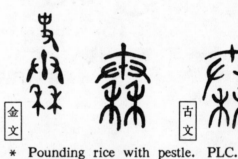 古文 篆文

— the Qin Dynasty (221—207 BC); a surname

嗪 qín; 蓁, 榛, 臻 zhēn.

* Pounding rice with pestle. PLC.   [舂 chōng: pound, 禾 hé: rice]

双手持杵舂米形。

sǎn

散 甲骨  金文 篆文

— to come loose; scattered.

撒 sā: to cast, let out, sǎ: to scatter, sprinkle, spill; 霰 xiàn; 散 sàn: to disperse.

* Shows a hand holding a tool used to peel off the outer fibers of a hemp plant.   [麻 má, 父 fù]

剥取麻类植物的表皮纤维。

bǐng 金文

稟

— to be endowed with; to report

to one's superior

懔 bǐng；凛，廪 lǐn.

古文 篆文

* A barn. PLC, 廪 lǐn: granary.

[禾 hé, 广 guǎng: shed.]

象谷仓之形。

▶ 稟的示意图。

sè 甲骨

啬 = 嗇

— stingy; miserly

墙，蔷，嫱，樯 qiáng；穑 sè.

篆文 古文 篆文

* A wheat silo. PLC, 穑 sè: (do) farm work.

[来 lái: pictograph of wheat]

象麦仓之形。

tú 甲骨

图 = 啚

— picture, chart; scheme,

plan, attempt; to pursue, seek;

intention

鄙 bǐ: small city, vulgar.

金文 篆文

* Perhaps it is the plan of a granary.

表示都鄙界划图形。懔、啬、墙、鄙等汉字都与粮仓有关，可能反映出收获以后大家的一些心态。

3.3   Domestication of Animals   驯化

The earliest animal to be domesticated by the early Chinese was probably the boar. The character 家 **jiā** (literally ″home″) may hint at the domestication process. In English, by comparison, the Latin root ″domus″ of domestication means ″house″. Perhaps, the modern use of 家 **jiā** came about as a result of the preliminary conditions which needed to be met before the domestication of animals could occur: the establishment of a durable shelter, the need for plenty of food, the use of fire and the development of hunting and agricultural skills.

中国古代青铜器铭文中有一种族徽图案(clan insignia)，为一人双手牵马，胯下有猪形。这一图形可能反映了先民驯化动物的经历，也是"家"字的字源。考古研究证明，公元前6000年到5700年，黄河流域的先民已经开始驯养猪、狗和鸡；长江流域在公元前5000年也出现了狗，猪和水牛等家畜。马的驯化可能迟至青铜时代。"家"源于驯化正与英文中的情况相反，"驯化"(domestication)一词的拉丁词根"domus"意为"房子"。只有在人类有了永久性的聚居点，打猎和农业得到发展从而获得更多的猎物和多余的粮食，才有可能开始驯养动物。

jiā
家 甲骨
— home
嫁：(of a woman) marry,
稼：to sow (grain)，镓 jià.

* 家 **jiā** depicts a man riding on or otherwise controlling a boar.　[大 dà，宀 mián，豕 shǐ]

野猪在房屋中形。一说象野猪在人胯下之形，表示驯化野猪，见大和豕字。

huàn
甲骨  篆文

豢
— to feed, keep.
卷 juǎn；卷，眷 juàn；拳
quán；眷 téng；券 quàn.

* The ancient pictographs show two hands catching a boar. The boar in the first pictograph is pregnant. In later forms of this character, the rice, 米 mǐ, was added to indicate the meaning of 豢 huàn：to feed. The upper part of this character is a radical implying the hands or the action of hands.　[子 zǐ, 豕 shǐ, 又 yòu and 舂 chōng]

　　抓获野猪用来驯化,篆文中加米指饲养之意。此字上部为一部件,表示双手及其动作。

zhuó
甲骨

椓
— to castrate, emasculate；beat
豖 zhǒng；琢，啄，逐 zhuó.

篆文 　参考

* The right-hand part of the character derives from an ancient drawing of a castrated boar.　[豕 shǐ]

　　象去势的猪形。

xiù
甲骨

臭
— odour, smell.
臭 chòu：ill-smelling；臭 or 嗅 xiù：to smell, scent, sniff at；溴 xiù.

篆文

* A combination of the pictographs of a nose and a dog. Since the dog has a keen sense of smell, the meaning of this character is very clear.　[自 zì, 犬 quǎn]

　　自(鼻子)和犬的组合。先民已经认识到了狗的嗅觉灵敏。

láo
甲骨

牢
— prison, jail；firm, fast, durable

金文 　篆文

* A corral for animals. Here, 宀 mián above 牛 niú: ox, indicates an enclosure.　[宀 mián, 牛 niú]

　　象兽栏之形。

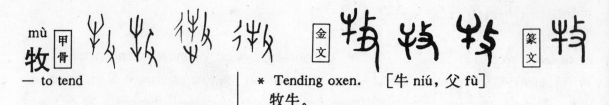

mù 牧 甲骨 金文 篆文
— to tend

* Tending oxen.   [牛 niú, 父 fù]
牧牛。

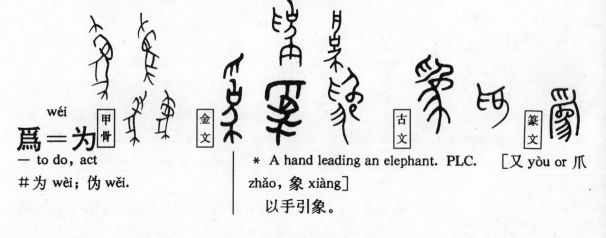

Rock painting • Tending sheep.
岩画・放牧图。内蒙狼山（自《世界美术史》第一卷 225 页）。

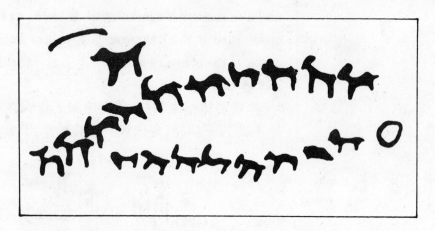

wéi 爲＝为 甲骨 金文 古文 篆文
— to do, act
＃为 wèi；伪 wěi.

* A hand leading an elephant. PLC.   [又 yòu or 爪 zhǎo, 象 xiàng]
以手引象。

chú 芻＝刍 甲骨 古文 篆文
— to chew; to cut grass; hay, fodder.
＃雏 chú；趋 qū；诌 zhōu；绉，
皱 zhòu；邹，驺 zōu.

* Shows a hand gathering grass for animal. (Cf. 反刍 **fǎnchú**: to ruminate; cud.)   [又 yòu, 艹 cǎo]
象用手收集草形。

dāo
甲骨
金文

篆文
刀
— knife
#切，氖，叨 dāo；叨 tāo；刁
diāo；倒 dǎo；到，倒 dào；钌，
招，昭 zhāo；沼 zhǎo；召，诏
zhào.

* Pictograph of an ancient bronze knife.
[刃 rèn，刂 as radical]
象古代青铜刀形。

rèn
甲骨
篆文

刃
— blade
#仞，纫，認＝认，轫，韧 rèn；
忍 rěn.

* The dot in this character was derived from the
blade of a knife to mark the cutting edge of the knife.
[刀 dāo]
刃字中的点源于表示刀刃部的线条。

▶ Pottery fragments with pictures of knives.
Shang period (*after Lindqvist*).
陶文·刀。

bā
甲骨
金文
古文
篆文

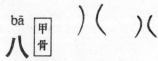
八
— eight
#扒，叭 bā；趴 pā；扒 pá.

* Derived from both the drawing of two separate
things and the sound of breaking. PLC. See below.
八表示一物分成两部分，也是借用了物体分裂开
的声音。

85

fēn

分 [甲骨] 丬丬 丬

[金文] 分 ﾉ少 少

[古文] 八 分

[篆文] 分

— to separate; divide, share; distinguish; a cent; a minute.

＃ 芬, 吩, 纷, 酚 fēn; 汾, 棼, 蚡 fén; 粉 fěn; 分, 份, 忿, 氛 fèn;（掰 = 擘 bāi）; 颁 bān; 扮 bàn; 岔 chà; 盼 pàn; 盆 pén; 贫 pín.

* A combination of 八 **bā** and 刀 **dāo**. Here, the knife element means "to cut"; 八 **bā** means something having been separated; thus, 分 **fēn** shows a knife cutting through or dividing something. ［八 bā, 刀 dāo］

分表示用刀将物剖分为两部分,"一分为二"。

▶ Inscriptions on some oracle bones with "八" and animals.

甲骨文所见从八之字。

bàn

半 [金文] 半 [古文] 半 半 [篆文] 半

— half, semi-; in the middle

＃ 判 pàn: to chop; 伴, 拌, 绊 bàn.

* A combination of 八 **bā**: a meaning element that indicates of cutting into separate parts, and 牛 **niú**: cow. ［八 bā, 牛 niú］

八与牛的组合。八有剖分的意思。

suí

㒸 [甲骨] 八 [篆文] 㒸

— archaic form of 遂 suí: to satisfy; then.

＃ 遂 suí; 隧, 燧, 邃, 燧 suì.

* A combination of 八 **bā**: a meaning element that indicates cutting into separate parts, and 豕 **shǐ**: boar PLC. ［八 bā, 豕 shǐ, 队 duì］

八与豕的组合,八有剖分的意思。

kè 刻

— to carve, inscribe; a quarter of an hour; petty; harshly

* A combination of a boar and a knife. 刻 kè shows a boar being slaughtered.　[亥 hài, 刀 dāo]

用刀宰猪之意。

mǎo 卯

— mortise; the fourth of the twelve Earthly Branches; (5 a. m. —7 a. m.); roll call

聊 liáo; 劉＝刘 liú: to kill, a surname; 柳 liǔ; 贸 mào; 泖, 峁, 昴, 铆 mǎo. (in ancient times, the sounds "m" and "l" were not distinguished)

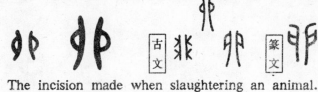

* The incision made when slaughtering an animal. PLC.

可能指屠宰牲畜的割口之形。

liú 留

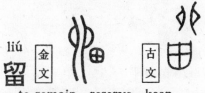

— to remain, reserve, keep.

榴, 瘤, 镏, 熘, 骝, 馏 liú; 溜, 熘 liū; 遛, 镏, 溜, 馏 liù.

* Combination of 卯 mǎo and 田 tián: a symbol for hunting (see also 番 fān and 畜 chù).

从田从卯。

jiě 解

— to separate; to solve

蟹, 懈, 解, 邂 xiè.

* An ox being butchered by hands, later with a knife.　[角 jiǎo: horn, 刀 dāo: knife, 牛 niú: ox, 爪 zhǎo or 又 yòu]

甲骨文解字表示以手解牛角之形,后在字形中用刀代替人手。

87

qí 奇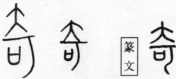

— strange, queer, rare; to surprise

\# 崎，骑 qí；绮 qǐ；奇，剞，犄，畸 jī；寄 jì；猗，漪 yī；倚，椅，旖 yǐ.

* A man riding a horse. The lower part 可 **kě** is an ancient phonetic element. PLC, 骑 **qí**: to ride, cavalry; with the radical 马 **mǎ**: horse.　［大 dà］

人骑马之形。

kè 克

— to restrain; to overcome; gram

\# 氪 kè.

* A cleaver with a handle for skinning animals, a flaying tool. PLC.

象剥皮工具形。传统的解释为象人肩形。

pí 皮

— skin; leather, hide; surface

\# 波，菠，玻 bō；跛，簸 bǒ；簸 bò；披 pī；陂，疲，铍 pí；坡，陂，颇 pō；婆 pó；破 pò.

* A hand holding a flaying tool.　［克 kè, 又 yòu］

手持剥皮工具形。或用手剥皮形。皮为部件多有波动意。

gé 革

— leather, hide; to change

* A spread-out hide of a flayed animal. The animal's head and tail are still attached to the hide. It is a radical in characters referring to leather.

象一张伸铺开的带有动物头和尾的兽皮。

Chapter 4

CRAFTSMANSHIP 手工业

To some extent, the characters in this chapter reflect certain feats of craftsmanship achieved in China 3000 years ago. However, China did not maintain her glory in the emergence of modern science and technology. In Chinese history, monarchs and philosophers only emphasized the skills of governing. From the Spring and Autumn Period (770－476 BC), Chinese intellectuals had a habit of "talking tall" and took a casual attitude towards engineering and technology. They themselves lacked a system of logic and a spirit inclined towards practical experimentation. As a sharp contrast, a lot of craftsmen were illiterate. They could neither read nor write complicated characters. Therefore, sometimes Chinese inventions were repeated. China's failure to develop technologically was associated with its feudal customs and closed society.

这一章的汉字在一定程度上能够反映出中国三千多年前在工程技术方面所取得的成就。但是,中国的知识分子从春秋战国以来,只知坐而论道,缺乏逻辑体系和实践精神;而大批有实践经验的手工艺人往往目不识丁。汉字本身的复杂性也是造成这一状况的原因之一。加之历代帝王只知"治人"的"南面之术"而不重视科学知识,使得中国人没能为近代科学的产生做出她应有的贡献。

4.1 Silk and Weaving 丝绸与纺织

The cultivation of the silkworm and the weaving of silk originated in China. Silk is the main Chinese contribution to the world's material civilization, and sericulture is a featuristic of Chinese civilization.

The earliest existing fragments of silk gauze, which belong to the Liangzhu culture dated about 3300－2200 BC, were discovered in Zhejiang Province in 1958. The silk was identified as that produced by domesticated silkworms. In the Han Dynasty the fine and brilliant material was traded and eagerly sought by the Romans, and later by the Byzantines. Having acquired a taste for such dress, they imported the silk and coveted the secret. At that time, an extensive trade was established along the routes through Central Asia to the West. Silk was the product which gave its name to this trade route, though it was not the only item in the trade. The trade was organized by officials in the form of government-sponsored caravans and made safe by the Chinese armies.

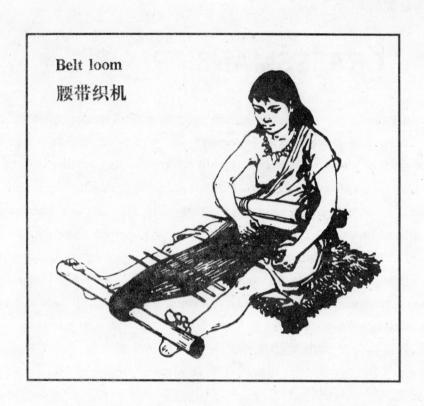

Belt loom
腰带织机

中国是全世界最早饲养家蚕和缲丝制绢的国家,而且长期以来曾经是从事这种手工业的唯一的国家。丝绸是中国对于世界物质文化最大的一项贡献。

中国最早的丝织品开始出现于中国东南的良渚文化*中,经商代到战国则已相当发达。由于在汉代画像石上出现了不少反映纺织的内容,人们对汉代的纺织业有了较详细的了解,著名的丝绸之路也是在汉代开辟的。但这部分汉字所反映的一些纺织工艺则要早于汉代。

suǒ 甲骨
索
— large rope; to search; a
surname
嗦 suǒ.

金文 | 古文 | 篆文

* A braided rope. The threads are hung and steadied with a H-shaped fixture.
象编好的绳索形。

---

* 良渚文化是指中国长江下游地区的新石器时代文化,因浙江省杭州市余杭县良渚遗址而得名,主要分布于太湖地区,年代为公元前 3300 年至前 2200 年。

zhuān 專＝专 甲骨 —special

砖 zhuān；转 zhuǎn；传,转,啭 zhuàn；传 chuán；團＝团,抟 tuán.

篆文

* A spindle being turned by a hand. PLC, 转 zhuǎn：to turn, change, transform；转 zhuǎn：to turn, revolve, rotate. ［又 yǒu or 寸 cùn］

用手旋转纺锤使三线捻成绳。

sāng 桑 甲骨 —mulberry

嗓,颡,操,磉 sǎng.

古文　篆文

* A mulberry tree with its leaves shown. Later, the "hands" in the treetop may represent picking the fresh leaves. A ton of leaves—leaves from thirty full-grown trees—are needed to produce five or six kilograms of silk, and of that probably only half can be used to make thread. ［木 mù, 又 yòu, 采 cǎi］

桑树形。

◀ Gathering mulberry leaves. This motif occurs on a bronze vessel. Warring States Period (475—221 BC).

战国铜器·采桑图。图中所绘桑树为经过人工改良的矮株的"地桑"或"鲁桑"。

shǔ 蜀 甲骨 — ancient name of Sichuan Province

金文　古文　篆文

觸＝触 chù；髑,独 dú；烛,躅 zhú；浊,镯 zhuó；屬＝属 shǔ；嘱,瞩,属 zhǔ.

* A silkworm with a big eye，目 mù. The 虫 chóng：worm-radical was a later addition. PLC.

象蚕之形。蚕本是一种害虫,在五千多年前中国人已开始驯养家蚕并利用蚕丝进行纺织。一个蚕茧的丝纤维长度能达到八百至一千米,其中雄性的蚕平均能比雌性的多吐丝一百米左右。

jīng

巠 = 全 金文

—warp, vertical textile

劲 jìn；径，茎，经 jīng；颈，到 jǐng；劲，径，胫，痉，经 jìng；羟 qiāng；轻，氢 qīng；烃 tīng.

* Drawing shows the organzine on a prehistoric belt or back-strap loom which was tied on one end around the weaver's waist and stretched at the other end by his or her feet. It is a common element in certain Chinese characters, indicating "straight" or "stretched".

象史前的一种腰带织机（腰机）。这种织机通常由两根平行杆支承经纱，一根固定在织布者的腰带上，另一根由织布者双脚蹬开以绷紧经纱。

jǐ

幾 = 几 金文

—nearly, almost

叽，饥，玑，讥，机，矶 jī.

* An ancient loom rigged with silk thread. PLC，機 = 机 jī：machine；the ancient loom was made of wood. [丝 sī：silk，人 rén，木 mù，几 jī]

古代纺织机的象形。

▶ Reproduction of a wooden loom, Han Dynasty (*after Wu, Cengde. p.* 29).

汉代织机复原图。

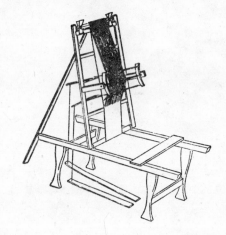

yǔ

予 古文 篆文

—to give, grant

予，预 yù；抒，纾 shū；序 xù；野 yě.

* Shows a shuttle which flies back and forth on the loom. PLC，杼 **zhù**：shuttle.

予表示（在织机上）飞动的梭子。

mì [甲骨] [金文] [篆文]

糸
—fine silk

＃ 絲＝丝：silk, mulberry silk，
𢇁，鸶 sī.

* A skein of silk. It is a radical for characters related to silk and weaving. [纟 as radical]

Most Chinese characters referring to color contain the silk-radical, an indication of the brilliance of the ancient material：红 **hóng**：red，绯 **fēi**：bright red，绛 **jiàng**：crimson，绿 **lù**：green，紫 **zǐ**：purple.

象束丝之形。

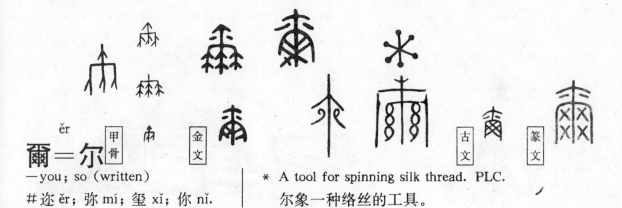

ěr [甲骨] [金文] [古文] [篆文]

爾＝尔
—you; so (written)

＃ 迩 ěr；弥 mí；玺 xǐ；你 nǐ.

* A tool for spinning silk thread. PLC.

尔象一种络丝的工具。

luàn [金文] [古文] [篆文]

亂＝乱
—in a mess; disorder; arbitrary

＃ 峦，孪，娈，挛，脔，銮，鸾
luán；变 biàn；恋 liàn；蛮 mán；
弯，湾 wān；辭＝辞 cí.

* Two hands arranging the dishevelled silk.
[爪 zhuǎ，又 yòu，糸 mì]

双手理丝形。乱字古代训治。

jiū [甲骨] [篆文]

丩
— (archiac character)

＃ 叫 jiào；纠，赳 jiū；收 shōu：
to gather, collect.

* Tangled silk. 纠 **jiū**：to entangle.

象(丝线)纠绕形。

4.2   Architecture   建筑

In China, the history of architecture can be traced back to two forms of dwellings——the cave-dwelling and the pile-dwelling. Remains of many prehistoric houses have been discovered; they are considered the prototypes of characteristic Chinese architecture.

中国的建筑史可能源于两种史前建筑形式——穴居和巢居。半地穴居址已有考古发现,它是由穴居发展而来的;而架空居住面的所谓"干栏式建筑"即巢居则比较难于留下什么遗迹。随着人类社会的发展,地面建筑逐渐成为建筑的主要形式,并发展为独具特色的中国建筑体系。

Neolithic wattle-and-daub dwellings, facing south and half-buried to avoid the icy winter winds. Banpo site.

半坡遗址建筑·半地穴居。

xuè 穴 篆文 参考

— a cave, cavern, grotto; a den; vital points recognized in acupuncture

* Drawing of a cave. The two dots indicate drops of water in the cave. This character is also a radical with the meaning of "cave" or "hole". [六 liù]

象洞穴形。两点指洞穴内的水滴。

shēn 罙 金文   篆文

—archaic form of 深 shēn；deep
琛 chēn；深 shēn；探 tàn.

* A hand exploring the inside of a cave. PLC, 探 **tàn**：to delve into. [穴 xuè，又 yòu，术 shù]

象用手探试洞穴深浅之形。

yǐ 乙 甲骨   金文   古文   篆文

—the second of the ten Heavenly Stems; second
钇 yǐ；（藝＝艺，億＝亿，憶＝忆 yì）.

* An ancient spade or billhook. It was borrowed to be used as one of the elements in the decimal counting cycle. [挖 wā：to dig；with a hand-radical and the meaning component 穴 xuè：cave]

乙可能象挖土的工具。传统的解释为象草木生长受阻委曲上出之形。

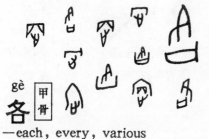
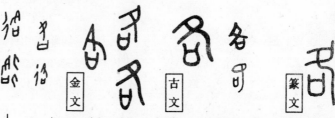

gè 各 甲骨   金文   古文   篆文

—each, every, various
铬 gè；搁，格，胳 gē；格，阁 gé；貉 hé，háo；咯 kǎ；客，恪 kè；落 là；烙，落，酪 lào；咯 lo；璐，鹭，露，路，赂 lù；略 lüè；洛，烙，落，络，骆 luò.

* A combination of the symbol of a foot and the symbol of a cave-dwelling. 各 **gè** implies a man entering the dwelling. PLC.

[客 kè：guest, and 止 zhǐ，出 chū，复 fù.]

各字上为足下为古代居穴，以足向居穴表示进入穴居。

chū
出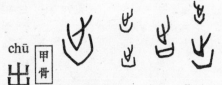
甲骨

—to go or come out; to exceed; to issue, put up; to arise, happen; to pay out; a dramatic piece

(础 = 礎 chǔ); 绌, 黜 chù; 咄 duō; 祟 suì; 拙 zhuō; 茁 zhuó; 屈 qū; 倔, 掘, 崛 jué; 倔 juè; 窟 kū.

金文 古文 篆文

* A combination of the symbol of a foot and the symbol of a cave-dwelling. 出 chū implies a man leaving the dwelling.   [各 gè and 止 zhǐ]

出字上为止下为古代居穴,以足背向穴居,表示自穴居外出。

---

fù
阜
甲骨

— mound; abundant

埠 bù.

篆文

* A flight of stairs. It is a radical for "moving up and down" which appears on the left side of some Chinese characters.   [降 jiàng, 阝 for radical, 邑 yì]

象阶梯之形。

---

yì
邑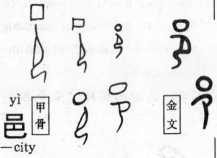
甲骨

—city

悒, 挹 yì; 扈, 滬 = 沪 hù.

金文 古文 篆文

* Recalls the settlement of early man. It is a radical for buildings which appears on the right side of some Chinese characters.   [阝 for radical, 阜 fù]

先人聚居之所。

---

yōng
邕
金文 篆文

—harmonious, peaceful; a city's name

癰 = 痈 yōng.

* A settlement near a river.

[川 chuān: river, 邑 yì: city]

近水而居。

liáng 甲骨
良
—good, fine

粮 liáng；踉 liàng；狼，锒，琅，郎，廊，螂 láng；朗 lǎng；浪 làng；娘 niáng；（釀 = 酿 niàng）.

金文 古文 篆文

* The foundation and porches of a prehistoric dwelling. PLC, 廊 **láng**：veranda.　[广 guǎng]

象半地穴居址。一说良象河流上架的桥梁 (liáng)形。

fù 甲骨
复
— to turn round, turn over；to duplicate；to compound, complex；to answer；again

復 = 复，腹，鳆，蝮，覆 fù；愎 bì；履 lǚ.

金文 篆文

* A foot and a prehistoric dwelling. It represented a man leaving the dwelling.　[良 liáng，止 zhǐ]

复表示人出入半地穴居室。

liù 甲骨
六
—six

陸 = 陆 lù，liù.

金文 古文 篆文

* A prehistoric house. The first pictograph (*) may be a drawing of a pile-dwelling. A common radical in characters related to the idea of "dwellings", 宀 **mián**, derived from these ancient pictographs；or perhaps it is a simplified form of 大 **dà**：a standing figure. [大 dà]

史前的地面建筑。"*"所画可能是指干栏式建筑。

Neolithic roundhouses, Banpo site.
半坡遗址圆形房子。

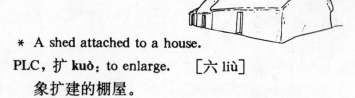

guǎng 金文 篆文

广

—wide; to expand

廣 = 广，犷 guǎng；矿，邝，旷 kuàng.

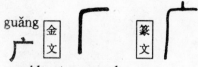

* A shed attached to a house.
PLC，扩 kuò：to enlarge.   [六 liù]
象扩建的棚屋。

xiàng 甲骨

向

—direction

饷，(響 = 响) xiǎng；垧，晌 shǎng.

金文   古文   篆文

* The window of a building.
房子的窗形。

shàng 甲骨

尚

— still；to esteem, value；a surname

赏 shǎng；绱 shàng；裳 shang；常，嫦，償 = 偿，嘗 = 尝，倘，裳 cháng；敞，廠 = 厂 chǎng；撑，瞠 chēng；當 = 当，档，铛 dāng；黨 = 党，说，挡 dǎng；棠，堂，膛，镗，螳 táng；倘，淌，躺，镋，耥，党 tǎng；趟 tàng；掌 zhǎng.

* Vapor or smoke issuing out from the window of a dwelling. PLC. [八 bā，向 xiàng，敞 chǎng：to open]
尚表示由窗口向上散气。

► Neolithic cave-dwelling, Banpo site.
半坡遗址建筑·地穴居。

yú 余
—I (written)

#餘＝余 yú；除，蜍 chú；荼，
塗＝涂，酴，途 tú；徐 xú；叙，
漵 xù.

* A shed with one center pole. PLC.

[舍 shě：shed, hut；compare the lower square element
with those of 高 gāo and 仓 cāng]

中间有柱子的栅舍。

gāo 高
—tall, high；of a high level or
degree；a surname

#篙，膏 gāo；藁，镐，缟，搞，稿
gǎo；嵩 sōng；敲 qiāo.

* A two story building.　　[京 jīng，享 xiǎng]

两层的楼房。

qiáo 喬＝乔
—tall；to disguise；a surname

#侨，荞，桥 qiáo.

* Derives from 高 gāo：high building, by adding
some strokes on the top of the building.　　[高 gāo]

乔是高的加划衍生字。

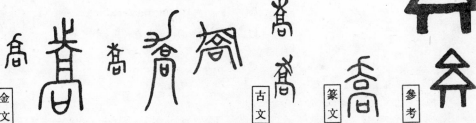

jīng 京
—the capital of a country

#惊，鲸 jīng；景，憬 jǐng；凉
liáng；谅，谅，晾 liàng；掠 lüè；
影 yǐng.

* A palatial structure.　　[高 gāo]

象宫殿一样高大的建筑。

Reproduction of a palace,
Western Zhou Dynasty
(*after Mao, Peiqi*).
西周宫殿建筑复原图(陕
西岐山凤雏村)。

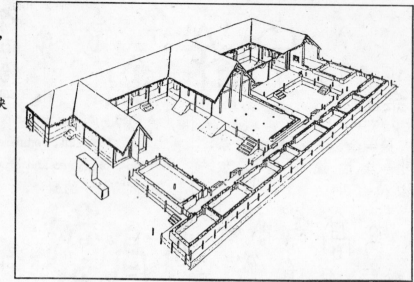

xiǎng
享 甲骨
—to enjoy
淳, 醇, 鹑 chún; 敦, 墩 dūn;
炖 dùn; 谆 zhūn.

金文   古文   篆文

* A structure built on a city wall, such as a tower over a city gate. PLC, 郭 **guō**: the outer wall of a city, with the city-radical, 邑 yì.   [廓 kuò: outline]
享象高台上的享堂建筑。

wǎ
瓦 篆文
—tile, slate; watt
瓦 wà: to tile.

* Two roof tiles. It is a radical for earthenware.
象房顶两片瓦俯仰相承形。一说象旋转的纺砖
(古称瓦)形。

cāng
倉=仓 甲骨
—storehouse, barn, granary
伧, 沧, 苍, 舱 cāng; 疮, 创
chuāng; 创, 怆 chuàng; 枪, 抢,
呛 qiāng; 抢 qiǎng; 呛, 炝, 跄
qiàng.

金文   古文   篆文

* A simple house with a door, 户 **hù**, and a stone step. Here, the upper "A" represents the roof of the storehouse.   [户 hù]
只有一扇门的简单房子。

庸 yōng [甲骨] [金文] [古文] [篆文]

— commonplace, mediocre; inferior, second-rate

#庸＝佣, 慵, 墉, 鳙, 镛 yōng.

* A city or palace with four gate towers. PLC, 墉 yōng: an adobe wall; small walled city. See above.

象四面建有城楼的城堡。

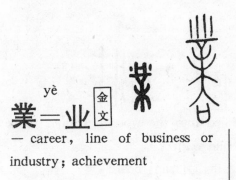

業＝业 yè [金文] [篆文]

— career, line of business or industry; achievement

* A pillar. PLC.

（古代悬挂乐器木架上的）支柱。

對＝对 duì [甲骨] [金文] [篆文]

— to set, adjust; right, correct; an answer, reply; mutual, face to face

#怼 duì.

* A hand erecting a pillar on the land.

[业 yè, 土 tǔ, 又 yòu or 寸 cùn]

象在地上用手树立起一根柱子。

The following four characters illustrate an ancient method of building walls by stamping earth between wooden frames.

下面四字可能反映了一种远古的建筑方法——版筑法。版筑法就是在拟筑的城墙内外两侧壁和向前延伸的一个横头处用横列木板堵成长方形板槽，然后在木板槽内逐层填土夯实。继之提高堵板，逐步加高和伸延以夯筑出墙体。这种建筑方法可能要早于商代中期，是由更为古老的夯筑法发展而来的。

jī 甲骨 金文 基 其 古文 坕 篆文

基
—foundation; basic, cardinal

* Combination of a bin, 其 **qí**, and earth, 土 **tǔ**. It implies earth being filled in a trench and tamped into forms for wall foundition. 其 **qí** is also a phonetic element.　[其 qí，土 tǔ]

用土筐向在地面上挖出的槽中填土，再经夯实形成基础。

zhuàng 金文 古文 壯 篆文 壯

壯＝壮
— strong, robust; magnifcent; to strengthen
＃莊＝庄，裝 zhuāng；奘 zhuǎng，zàng（玄奘）.

* Earth being filled into the wooden frames to be compacted into a solid wall.
[裝 zhuāng：to fill in，爿 pàn：board]
（用土筐）向板槽中装土。

gōng 甲骨 工 金文 工 工 古文 工 篆文 工

工
—labour, work; worker; skill; be good at
＃攻，红，功 gōng；汞 gǒng；贡 gòng；扛，肛，缸 gāng；杠 gàng；红，虹 hóng；讧 hòng；江，豇 jiāng；扛 káng；项 xiàng.

* A wood tamper, or mallet.
象夯杵之形。

gǒng 金文 篆文 巩

鞏＝巩
—to consolidate; a surname
＃恐 kǒng；跫 qióng；築＝筑 zhù：to build.

* A man pounding the earth with a tamper. Here, 工 **gōng** is also a phonetic element.　[工 gōng：tamper]
人手持夯杵。

4.3　Pottery Making and Metallurgy　陶冶

4.3.1—Pottery Making　制陶

▶ Reproduction of two Neolithic kilns, Banpo site.
半坡遗址陶窑复原图。

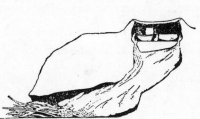

After the glaciers of the Ice Age retreated, clay and pottery-making surfaced. Thus, pottery is often identified with the Neolithic culture in China. Certain potsherds dating back as far as 10,000 years ago have been found in Guangxi Province.

　　陶器的出现是人类从旧石器时代进入到新石器时代的重要标志。中国有着悠久的制陶历史。在中国广西出土过距今约一万年的陶片,这是目前已知有关中国制陶史的最早记录。

táo 匋 [金文]  [古文] [篆文]

— ancient form of 陶 táo: pottery.

淘,陶,萄 táo; 掏 tāo.

* A potter pounding clay in a container with a pestle.
[人 rén, 午 wǔ]
　　象陶工持杵捣泥形。

fǒu 缶 [甲骨] 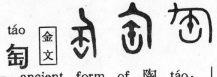 [金文] [古文] 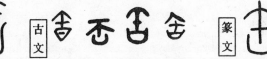 [篆文]

— an amphora-like jar

窑 yáo: kiln.

* The pestle and the container in character 陶 táo (see above). It is a radical for earthenware.
[午 wǔ, 陶 táo]
　　陶字中的杵与容器。

gōng 公 [甲骨] 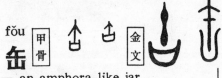 [金文] 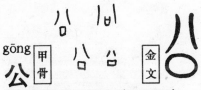 [古文] [篆文]

— public; male (animal); a surname

蚣 gōng; 松, 松, 淞, 菘 sōng; 讼, 颂 sòng; 松 zhōng; 翁, 嗡, 蓊 wēng; 滚 gǔn.

* Generally supposed to be a drawing of an earthen jar. PLC, 瓮 wèng: urn.
　　象瓮口之形。也可能表示公平分物之意,参见八。

4. 3. 2—Metallurgy   冶金

In view of the Chinese bronze culture, the characters derived from metallurgy are limited. The reason may be that bronze-casting was a special technique used for making weapons and ritual vessels which were imperative for governing. Common people could not duplicate the process of metallurgy.

"国之大事,在祀与戎"。在中国的商周时代,青铜主要用来制造维护国家统治的工具——祭器与兵器,一般人不易了解青铜冶炼与铸造方面的技术。因此,反映原始冶金技术的文字出现较迟,数量也有限。

Chinese bronze vessels.
中国青铜器。

鼎 dǐng

方鼎

鬲 lì

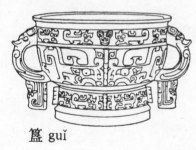
簋 guǐ

盂 yú

匜

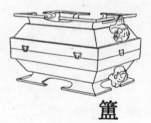
簠

方彝 fāng yí

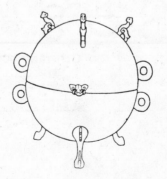
敦 duì

豆 dòu

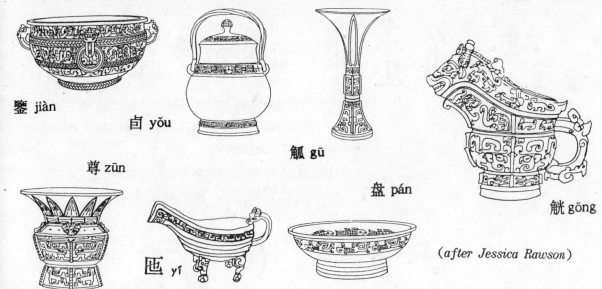

鉴 jiàn

卣 yǒu

尊 zūn

觚 gū

盘 pán

匜 yí

觥 gōng

(*after Jessica Rawson*)

---

duàn
段 金文 篆文

— section; stage; a surname
缎，椴，煅，锻 duàn.

* A hand holding a tool to dig ore. PLC, 锻 **duàn**: to forge.　　[厂 hàn，殳 shū]

象人手持工具在崖边凿取矿石。

---

jiǎ
叚 金文 古文 篆文

— ancient form of 假 jiǎ: false; to borrow.
假 jiǎ, jià; 蝦＝虾 xiā; 遐，瑕，暇，霞 xiá.

* Two hands obtaining ore from a quarry. PLC.
[厂 hàn，又 yòu]

双手取矿石形。

---

bīng
仌 甲骨 金文 古文 篆文 参考 冰

— (archaic character)
金 jīn; 冶 yě: to smelt (metal).

* Two bronze ingots. It is a radical referring to coldness, because of the feeling of touching the bronze.
[冰 bīng: ice]

象两块圆饼状的铜锭形。

105

jīn
金
— gold; bronze
衔 xián; 鑫 xīn.

* A combination of arrowhead and and an ax, both of them are made of bronze. The two dots represent bronze ingots, see above.
[入 rù, 王 wáng, 冫 bīng 乍 as radical.]
金字头象青铜箭头,两点表示铜锭。

fán
凡
— commonplace, ordinary; this mortal world, the earth; every, any, all
(矾＝礬), 钒 fán; 帆 fān; 犯, 梵 fàn.

* A molding box with four carrying bars. PLC.
[范 fàn: model, pattern, limits]
凡象铸金属件的范模。传统的解释为象盘形。

Iron casting, rubbing from a stone relief showing a round bellows and iron forging. Han Dynasty, excavated from a tomb in Shandong Province (*after Wu, Cengde. p. 25*).
汉画像石·冶铁图。山东腾县宏道院出土。

tóng
同
— same, alike, similar; to be the same as; together; and
垌,茼,峒,桐,酮,铜 tóng; 筒 tǒng; 侗,垌,恫,峒,洞,胴,硐 dòng; 興＝兴 xīng.

* A combination of 凡 **fán** and 口 **kǒu**. 凡 **fán** is a drawing of a molding box; thus, the meaning of 同 **tóng** derives from the idea "same castings".
[凡 fán, 口 kǒu]
同字从口从凡。

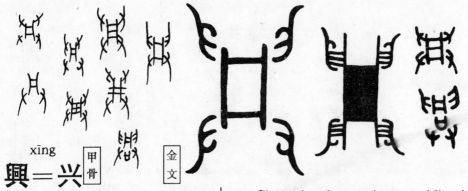

xīng 興=兴 [甲骨] [金文] [篆文]
— to get up, rise; to prosper, prevail; to promote

* Shows hands carrying a molding box.
[同 tóng, 舁 yù]
四手抬起范模。

yě 冶 [金文] [篆文]
— to smelt (metal)

* Depicts the melting of bronze ingots. 台 **yí** is a phonetic element. [冫 bīng, 火 huǒ, 台 yí]
冶表示冶炼铜锭。

zé 則=则 [金文] [古文] [篆文]
— criterion; rule; to imitate (written); however
侧 测, 恻, 厕 cè; 铡 zhá.

* To carve a pattern for the molding and casting of bronze vessel. [鼎 dǐng, 贝 bèi, 刀 dāo]
按照一件鼎仿制雕刻另一件鼎的铸范。

zhù 鑄=铸 [甲骨] [金文] [古文] [篆文]
— to cast, to mint

* The ancient pictographs for "casting" are delicate and complicated; the modern character 铸 **zhù** is a pictophone with the metallurgy-radical and 寿 **shòu**, an ancient phonetic element. [金 jīn, 又 yòu, 火 huǒ]
浇铸象形。后铸字改为形声。

4.4   Woodworking and Lacquer   木工与漆艺

4.4.1—Woodworking   木工

xiāng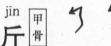

相

— to observe, look at; to watch for; a surname; mutually; together

厢,湘,箱 xiāng；想 xiǎng；霜,孀 shuāng.

* To look at a tree and judge its worth.

［木 mù，目 mù，相 xiàng：looks, to look at and judge］

察看木料。

jīn

斤

— jīn, a unit of weight (＝1/2 kg)

近 jìn；祈,圻,蕲,颀 qí；芹 qín；欣,忻,昕 xīn；斫 zhuó.

* An ax with a crooked handle. PLC，斧 fǔ：ax；with the pictophonetic element：父 fù.

［父 fù，两 liǎng］

一种曲柄斧的象形。

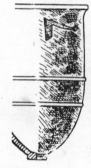

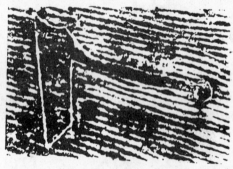

◀ Adze on a clay vessel from *Dawenkou*, Neolithic period (*after Lindqvist*).

陶文·斤。山东大汶口出土。

kě

可

— may, can; to approve

岢,坷 kě；坷,苛,珂,柯,疴,钶,轲,轲 kē；可 kè；阿,锕 ā；啊 ā, á, ǎ, à；阿,屙,婀 ē；呵 hē；何,河,荷 hé；哥,歌 gē.

* Drawing shows the handle of an ax, and a square which was used to differentiate this pictograph from other ancient words such as 乃 nǎi. PLC，柯 kē；ax-handle；with a wood-radical.   ［斤 jīn］

象斤斧的曲柄。

xī 析 甲骨

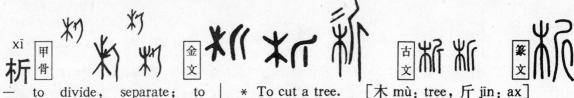 金文 古文 篆文

— to divide, separate; to analyse, dissect, resolve

\# 淅, 晰, 蜥 xī.

* To cut a tree. [木 mù: tree, 斤 jīn: ax]

用斤斧砍伐树木。

zhé 折 甲骨

— to break, snap; to suffer the loss of; to convert into

\# 哲, 蜇 zhé; 淅 zhè; 折 shé; 逝, 誓 shì.

 金文 古文 篆文

* To cut down a tree. Here, the hand radical was incorrectly derived from the broken trunk. [析 xī]

以斤砍断树木。

zhí 直 甲骨 金文 古文 篆文

— straight; vertical; just, upright; to straighten; direct; continuously

\# 值, 植, 殖 zhí; 置 zhì; 矗 chù; 德 dé: virtue, morals; 聽 =听 tīng.

* Ancient forms of 直 zhí portray an eye gazing at a straight line or rule. [目 mù]

以目视测一直物形。

dīng 丁 甲骨

 金文 古文 篆文

— small cubes; man, population; the fourth of the ten Heavenly stems

\# 仃, 叮, 玎, 盯, 町, 钉, 疔, 耵, 酊 dīng; 酊, 顶 dǐng; 订, 钉 dìng; 打 dǎ, dá; (燈=灯 dēng); 汀, (廳=厅) tīng; 亭, 停, 葶, 婷 tíng; 町 tǐng.

* A nail. PLC, 钉 dīng: nail, tack; with a metal-radical.

象钉形。

piàn
片 [篆文]
— a flat, thin piece

* Shows a chopped wood. This character is the right-hand part of 木 mù：tree. PLC.　[木 mù, 爿 pán]
象析木形。

méi
枚 [甲骨] [金文] [篆文] [参考]
— stem；piece of stick used as mouth gag；a countable piece；a surname

* To plane or cut a piece of wood with a tool.
[木 mù, 父 fù]
用工具修整树干。

yú
俞 [金文]
— a surname
渝,愉,揄,逾,瑜,榆,舰,蝓,窬,崳 yú；谕,喻,愈 yù；觎,输 shū；偷 tōu.

* To carve a canoe with a chisel or knife. PLC.
[舟 zhōu, 刀 dāo]
用工具制作木舟。俞为部件多有"空"意。

jǔ
矩 [金文] [古文] [篆文]
— carpenter's square；rule, regulation

* A carpenter using a ruler. The 矢 shǐ：arrow, was a modification of the similar 夫 fū：man. See below.
[夫 fū]
人手持矩形。

jù
巨 [金文] [古文] [篆文]
— huge
拒,苣,炬,距 jù；矩,柜 jǔ；渠 qú.

* The hand and the ruler from the character 矩 jǔ, see above. PLC.
矩字中的尺矩形。

110

4. 4. 2—Lacquerwork 漆艺

The lacquer tree is a kind of Oriental tree. Its sap, lacquer, can be used to make lacquerware. The history of lacquerwork in China goes back to the earliest legends of Chinese history. The art was taken to Japan from China via Korea in the middle of the 6th century. During the same period, the lacquer tree was also introduced to Japan. European craftsmen in the 18th and 19th centuries also copied the technique of making lacquerware.

Lacquer itself, in its natural state, is a thick, syrupy whitish or grayish sap that turns dark brown or black when oxidized. The sap must undergo special preparation before it is ready to be used. First it is purified, then it is stirred until liquefied. Afterwards it is heated and stored in an airtight container until required for use. The base to which lacquer is applied is usually wood, sometimes animal skins or gunny cloth. In order to become as hard as possible, lacquer must "dry" in a damp atmosphere with plenty of moisture. This requirement led to the development of special techniques for hardening lacquerware.

Like oil painting and sculpture, lacquer painting is one form of art in China. The different colors of lacquer are mixed by the addition of different substances, such as cinnabar for red. Greens, dull yellow, brown, black, and purple are other possible colors. Gold, silver, engraving, carving, and inlay have all been used to create decorative effects of extreme richness. Both Chinese and Japanese craftmen favor shell inlays such as mother-of-pearl and egg-shells. Jade, ivory, porcelain and coral inlays are also used. The lacquer itself is a very good adhesive.

Like poison ivy, natural lacquer is highly irritating to the skin, but the finished product has no harmful effects.

同丝绸的发明一样,漆艺是中国人对世界物质文明的又一项重要贡献。
生漆是从漆树割取的天然液汁,主要由漆酚、漆酶、树胶质及水分构成。用它作涂料或制作漆器,不仅光彩照人,而且具有耐潮、耐高温、耐腐蚀等特殊功能。中国人使用漆的历史可上溯到新石器时代。浙江余姚河姆渡文化(公元前 5000 年)出土有一件据认为是涂有朱红色漆的木碗;山西襄汾陶寺龙山文化(公元前 2000 年左右)遗址中也出土一批外表涂料为漆类物的木器。自商周到秦汉漆与漆器制作技术得到很大发展,应用非常广泛。商代的漆器中已经出现漆绘雕花和镶嵌等工艺。春秋时代人们已经重视漆树的栽培。据史书记载,战国时期的庄子,曾经在蒙地当过漆园吏。《史记·滑稽列传》中还有关于利用"阴室"在潮湿环境下使漆易于干固的记载。在汉代中国的漆树和漆器制作技术就已经流传到亚洲一些国家。西方人多认为漆器制作源于日本,实际上,漆艺和漆树是在公元六世纪中叶经朝鲜传到日本的,在十八至十九世纪欧洲人也掌握了这门技术。

　　漆器的胎一般使用木、皮、麻布等材料。天然的漆在使用前要经过过滤和氧化处理。用多种矿物性和植物性染料可调制出各种颜色的漆。由于漆本身就是很好的粘合剂（中国有成语"如胶似漆"），而且多层涂层厚度和硬度都非常适于镶嵌和雕刻，同时镶嵌还能补充漆色的不足，如用蛋壳镶嵌可替代不易调制出的白色漆，因此利用漆制作工艺或美术作品有很强的表现力。在中国，同油画和雕塑一样，漆画被认为是艺术形式之一。

　　生漆有毒性。干漆可入药，有破瘀的功效。古人曾错误地认为干漆是中药中的延年上品。

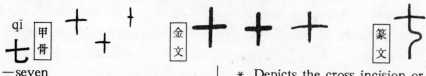

qī　甲骨　金文　篆文
七
—seven
＃ 柒 qī.

* Depicts the cross incision or crosscut made in a tree for tapping the lacquer. PLC.　［汁 zhī：juice，十 shí］

The Japanese tap lacquer trees once in every ten years, between June and September. The most plausible reason for the inferiority of Chinese to Japanese lacquer seems to be related to the sap-gathering techniques. The Chinese tap the lacquer tree at any time, while the Japanese do it when the sap is at its best.

象漆树上取漆的切口形，柒是七的大写。

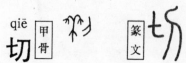

qiē　甲骨　篆文
切
— to cut, slice, incise
＃ 沏 qī；砌 qì；切，（窃＝竊）qiè；（彻＝徹 chè）.

* A combination of 七 qī and a knife.
［七 qī：cross incision，刀 dāo：knife］
切从七从刀。

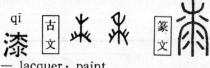

qī　古文　篆文
漆
— lacquer; paint
＃ 膝 qī, xī.

* A lacquer tree with the lacquer sap (the dots) flowing down. The left liquid-radical is a later addition.　［木 mù，水 shuǐ］
象漆从漆树中流下。

lǜ 率 [甲骨]

— rate, proportion ratio

率,蟀 shuài；摔 shuāi.

[金文] [古文] [篆文]

* Putting natural lacquer in a cloth sack, and then wringing out purified lacquer.

[糸 mì, 水 shuǐ, 又 yòu]

将生漆倒入布袋进行绞拧,滤去杂质。

4.5 Making Wine 酿酒

Unlike Europe's method of making wine, early Chinese used wine leaven and grain to make "rice wine". The Chinese method is called the "amylomyces process".

In 1949, two Shang Dynasty brewery sites were found at *Erligang* in Henan Province, and *Taixi* Village, *Gaocheng* County, Hebei Province. However, the earliest wine found in China belongs to the Warring States Period, dated about 2000 years ago. In 1974, two kinds of wine were found in the Prince of Zhongshan's tomb in Hebei Province. One was green and transparent, the other was dark green. When excavated, both pots of wine were tightly sealed with rust. But on opening the pots, a fragrance of wine filled the room. Scientists believe that this wine was made by fermentation of yeast.

"清酏之美,始于耒耜"。中国人在农业起源时期已经开始酿酒了,也就是说中国人用霉菌酿酒已有六、七千年的历史。中国古代的酒是用酒曲和谷物发酵而酿成的。这种酿酒的方法为"淀粉霉法",它与西方的酿酒方法是不同的。

Bronze wine cups, Zhou period.

青铜酒杯。

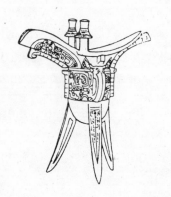
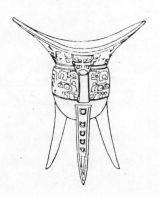
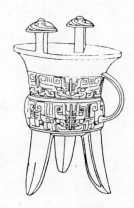

qūn

—barn

麇 qún；菌 jūn.

* Rice stored in a sealed container or barn. Cf. 菌 **jūn**: fungus, bacterium.   [禾 hé：rice]

封存谷物。先民曾受到发霉发芽的谷物所产生的天然酒曲的启发，从而发明出酿酒的方法。

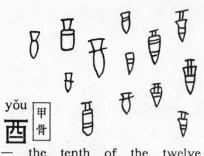

yǒu

— the tenth of the twelve Earthly Branches

酒 jiǔ.

* A wine jug. PLC, 酒 jiǔ：wine. 酉 **yǒu** is a radical for characters associated with wine and fermenting.

象酒罐形。

chàng

— a sacrificial wine

鬱＝郁 yù.

* A kettle containing wine leaven.   [皂 zào]

象盛放有发酵醪的容器。鬯也指酿酒用的香草。

qiú

— chief of a tribe; chieftain

遒 qiú；猶＝犹，蝤，猷 yóu.

* A wine jug with a perforated lid that is filtering the sediment from wine leaven. PLC.   [酉 yǒu]

酋上置一容器，内盛发酵醪。后省为两点，多解释为"酒香"。

yóu

— cause, reason; due to ; by through; to obey; from
笛，迪 dí；(邮＝邮)，油，铀，柚，蚰 yóu；柚，釉，鼬 yòu；抽 chōu；轴，妯 zhóu；宙，胄，轴 zhòu；袖，岫 xiù.

* A filtering sack. PLC. 由 **yóu** is an element with the meaning of "hole" or "perforated" by. its extended meaning of "filtering" in certain derivatives.
象滤酒的囊形。

tán 覃 〔金文〕
— deep (written); a surname
潭，谭 tán；蕈 xùn.

〔篆文〕

* A wine vessel with a cover. PLC.
象酒器上有封盖。

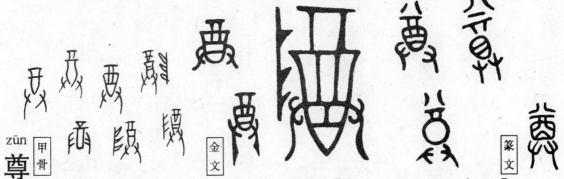

zūn 尊 〔甲骨〕 〔金文〕 〔篆文〕
— to respect, revere, venerate; venerable, honorable; a title of respect; an ancient wine vessel

* To toast.　〔酋 qiú, 又 yòu or 寸 cùn〕
双手捧酒尊敬酒。

diàn 奠 〔甲骨〕 〔金文〕 〔古文〕 〔篆文〕
— to establish, settle; make offerings to the spirits of the dead
鄭＝郑 zhèng；掷 zhì, zhī；踯 zhí.

* Shows the offering of a wine jug. The lower stroke indicates the base.　〔酋 qiú〕
象置酒尊于基荐上。

jué 甲骨 金文 篆文

爵

— an ancient wine vessel with three legs and a loop handle; the rank of nobility, peerage

嚼，爝 jué, jiào；嚼 jiáo.

* Shows a hand holding a *jue*.

[皀 zào，又 yòu or 寸 cùn]

手持饮酒爵形。

fú 甲骨 金文 古文 篆文 参考 福 富

畐

— full (archaic)

逼 bī；蔔，幅，福，蝠，辐 fú；副，富 fù.

* A wine jar. PLC.

[福 fú：good fortune，富 fù：rich，酉 yǒu]

象大酒缸之形。

lù 甲骨 金文 古文 禄 篆文

录

— collection；record；to copy；to employ

渌，逯，绿，禄，碌 lù；绿 lù；碌 liù.

* Drawing of a hanging sack used for filtering wine. The lower element is 水 **shuǐ**：water.

[索 suǒ，由 yóu]

酒从挂起来过滤(lù)酒的袋中滤出。

Chapter 5

LIVELIHOOD   日常生活

5.1   The Use of Fire   火的使用

Some charred animal bones, the remnants of an early Chinese repast, were found in Xihoudu, a Paleolithic site dated 1,800,000 years ago. This is the earliest evidence of the use of fire by man on earth.

在中国已知最早的旧石器时代遗存——西侯度文化*中发现有被火烧过的兽骨，目前这是在世界范围内最早的人类用火遗迹。这一发现也大大提前了人类用火的历史。

huǒ 火 甲骨 古文 篆文 参考 炎
— fire; anger, temper; internal heat——one of the six causes of disease
＃伙，钬 huǒ；灰 huī；炎 yán；淡，啖，氮 dàn；痰，谈 tán；毯 tǎn；剡 yǎn，shàn；秋 qiū.

* A flame. There are three forms of the ″fire″ radical in many Chinese characters：one is placed on the left side of a character；the others are lower radicals written as a flattened 火 **huǒ** or as four dots.
象火焰形。

fén 焚 甲骨 金文 篆文
— to burn

* A forest on fire.   [林 lín：forest, 火 huǒ：fire]
焚烧树林，用以驱兽围猎或开辟农田。

* 中国华北地区旧石器时代早期文化，发现于山西省芮城县西侯度村附近，其年代初步测定为距今 180 万年。

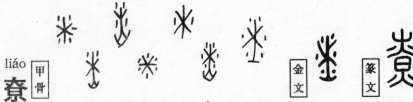

liáo 燎 [甲骨]
— ancient form of 燎 liáo: to burn

燎 lǎo；撩 liāo；療＝疗，遼＝辽，僚，寮，撩，鹩，嘹，獠，燎，缭 liáo；潦，瞭＝了，燎 liǎo；瞭＝了，镣 liào.

* A bonfire. The upper dots in this character represent sparks, and the bottom 小 xiǎo derives from 火 huǒ: fire.   [木 mù, 燎 liǎo: to singe]
象一堆篝火之形。

熱＝热 [甲骨]
rè
— hot

* A man holding a torch. PLC. In spite of pictorial similarity, this character has nothing to do etymologically with 藝＝艺 yì which is descended from the drawing of a man planting.   [执 zhí]
象人手持火把之形。

叟 [甲骨]
sǒu
— old man

溲，搜，艘，馊，飕 sōu；嫂 sǎo；瘦 shòu.

* A hand holding a torch to search a house. PLC, 搜 sōu: to search; with a hand-radical.   [又 yòu]
象人手持火把在屋内搜索之形。

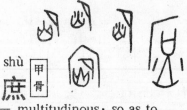 

庶 [甲骨] [金文] [古文] [篆文]
shù
— multitudinous; so as to

遮 zhē；蔗，鹧 zhè；摭 zhí.

* A pebble being heated over fire, later to be put in a pot to heat water, an ancient cooking technique. PLC. [石 shí, 火 huǒ, 者 zhě]
庶表示以火烧石。

huī
灰
— ash; gray
恢，诙 huī；盔 kuī；炭：
charcoal，碳：carbon tàn；羰
tāng.

* Something being picked up from a fire. The semantic link would have been "ash".
[又 yòu：hand，火 huǒ：fire]
灰表示用手从火中取出之物，即灰炭。

lú
盧＝卢
— a surname
廬＝庐，芦，炉，胪，舻，轳，
颅，鸬，鲈 lú；驴 lú.

* An ancient stove. The upper part, the "tiger's head", is a phonetic element. PLC, 爐＝炉 lú：stove；with a fire radical.   [虎 hǔ，皿 mǐn，火 huǒ]
象古代火炉之形。

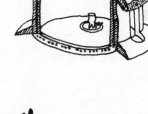

▶ A wattle-and-daub house with an earthenware stove in its centre. Neolithic period.
河南龙山文化 11 号木骨垛泥墙白灰面圆形房（采自《中国大百科全书.考古学》，204 页）。

guāng
光
— light，ray；brightness，lustre，glory，honour；glossy，polished；bare，naked；only，merely；used up
胱 guāng；桄 guàng；觥 gōng；恍，晃，幌 huǎng；晃 huàng.

* A combination of 火 huǒ：fire, and 人 rén or 卩 jié：a kneeling figure.   [火 huǒ，卩 jié]
光从火在人上。

chì
赤
— red; loyal; bare

＃ 哧 chī; 赫 hè; 赭 zhě.

* A combination of 大 **dà**: a standing man, and 火 **huǒ**: fire.   [大 dà, 火 huǒ]

赤从大从火。

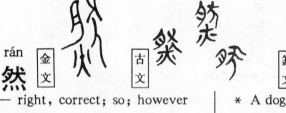

rán
然
— right, correct; so; however

＃ 燃 rán.

* A dog being roasted over fire. PLC, 燃 **rán**: ignite.

[犬 quǎn, 火 huǒ, 肉 ròu]

象烧烤犬之形。

jiāo
焦
— burnt, scorched; coke; a surname

＃ 礁, 蕉, 鹪 jiāo; 噍 jiào; 憔,
谯, 瞧, 樵 qiáo; 蘸 zhàn.

* A bird being roasted over fire.

[隹 zhuī: bird, 火 huǒ: fire]

象烧烤鸟之形。

gāo
羔
— lamb, kid, fawn

＃ 糕 gāo: cake, pudding; 羹
gēng: a thick soup.

* A lamb being roasted over fire. Or the lower four dots derive from 少 **shào**, thus, this character is a combination of 羊 **yáng** and 少 **shào** or 小 **xiǎo**.

[羊 yáng, 火 huǒ, 小 xiǎo]

象烧烤羊之形。

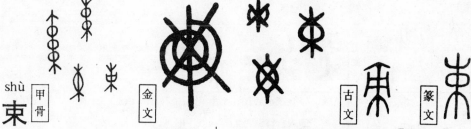

親＝亲 qīn

— blood relation, relative; parent; marriage; close, intimate; to kiss; in person

＃榇＝梫,襯＝衬 chèn；新,薪 xīn.

* A pictophone. It indicates firewood. PLC. 薪 xīn: firewood.

[辛 xīn: phonetic element, 木 mù: tree, 斤 jīn: ax]
从木辛声,表示柴薪。

束 shù

— to bind, tie; control, restrain; bundle, bunch, sheaf; a surname

＃敕 chì；辣 là；嫩 nèn；悚,竦 sǒng；速,觫,涑,薻,簌 sù.

* A bundle of firewood. [木 mù]
象一捆柴禾之形。

困 kùn

— to be stranded, be hard pressed; to surround, pin down

＃悃,捆,阃 kǔn；睏＝困 kùn.

* Firewood corded up. PLC, 捆 kǔn: to tie, bundle up, bundle. [木 mù]
困表示捆扎木柴。

5.2   Cooking and Eating   饮食

dòu
豆 甲骨   金文

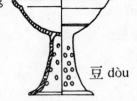
古文   篆文

— an ancient stemmed bowl; bean

逗，痘 dòu；登 dēng；短 duǎn；頭＝头 tóu.

* A Chinese vessel, consisting of a tall base stem supporting a bowl or platter.

一种古代的食具。

豆 dòu

sháo
勺 甲骨   金文   篆文

— spoon, scoop

芍 sháo；豹 bào；的 dì, dè；钓 diào；妁 shuò；约 yāo, yuē；(药＝藥) yào；哟 yō, yo；灼，酌 zhuó.

* A ladle with something (the dot) in it. [斗 dǒu] 象勺中盛物（一点）形。

dǒu
斗 甲骨   金文

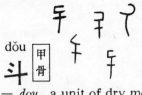   
古文   篆文

— *dou*, a unit of dry measure for grain (＝1 decalitre); the Big Dipper

抖，蚪 dǒu；斛，槲 hú；戽 hù；科，蝌 kē；魁 kuí；料 liào：to expect.

* A vessel with a long handle. The stroke on the handle indicates that this character was borrowed as a unit of measurement.   [斗 dòu, 一 yī] 象有柄的容器。

shēng
升 甲骨   金文   古文   篆文

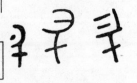

— *sheng*, a unit of dry measure for grain (＝1 litre); litre (l.); to rise, hoist, ascend; to promote

* Meting out rice with a *dou* measure. PLC. [斗 dǒu] 用斗量米。

dǐng 鼎 甲骨 金文 古文 篆文

— an ancient cooking vessel with two loop handles and three or four legs, a tripod

* Pictograph. In certain characters, 贝 **bèi** is the simplified form of 鼎 **dǐng**. [员 yuán，贞 zhēn]

象一种三足的煮肉的锅，四足的鼎称为方鼎。

yuán
员＝员 甲骨 金文 篆文

— member of staff

#圆 yuán；损 sǔn；员，郧 yún；
陨，殒 yǔn；员 yùn.

* The upper 口 **kǒu** indicates the round lip of a tripod. PLC, 圆 **yuán**：round, a circle.

[口 kǒu，鼎 dǐng：tripod]

员字上面的"口"表示鼎的圆形上口沿。

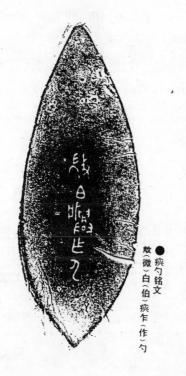

●疢勺铭文
敔（微）白（伯）疢乍（作）勺

◀ Rubbing of inscriptions on a bronze spoon, West Zhou Dynasty.

西周青铜勺铭文。一九七六年出土于陕西省扶风县（采自陈全方《周原与周文化》）。

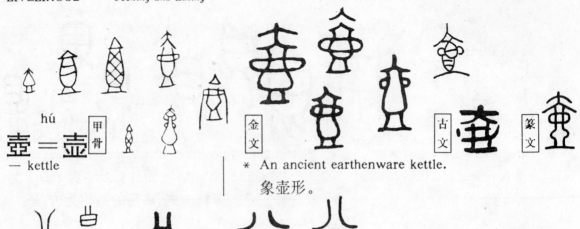

hú 壺 = 壶 〔甲骨〕
— kettle

* An ancient earthenware kettle.
象壶形。

céng 曾 〔甲骨〕〔金文〕
— yet

＃ 曾，增，憎，缯，罾 zēng；缯，甑，赠 zèng.

* A prehistoric earthenware pot used for steaming food; the upper 八 **bā** stands perhaps for the emerging vapour. PLC, 甑 **zèng**: steamer; with an earthenware-radical, 瓦 **wǎ**. The steamer has a perforated bottom to allow steam to rise, and it is placed on an earthenware tripod, the 鬲 **lì**.
〔增 zēng：to add，increase，鬲 lì〕

　　曾表示在鬲上增加一个底部有孔的甑，形成一种蒸（zhēng）锅。曾字上面的"八"可能表示蒸气。

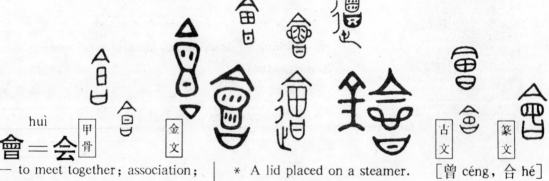

huì 會 = 会 〔甲骨〕〔金文〕
— to meet together; association; meeting; can, will

＃ 荟，烩，绘 huì；刽，桧 guì；会，侩，狯，脍，郐，哙，浍 kuài.

* A lid placed on a steamer.
会字表示在甑上加盖。

〔曾 céng，合 hé〕

hé

合

— close; to join, combine; whole; proper

#盒,颌 hé；答,搭,嗒,褡 dā；答 dá；鸽 gē；蛤,拼,阁 gé；合 gě；给 gěi,jǐ；哈,铪 hā；蛤 há；洽,恰 qià；拾 shí.

* An earthenware pot with a lid.　[会 huì]

陶锅有盖,上下相合。

jiāng

将＝将

— to take care of (one's health) (written)；support (written)；do sth.；egg on；be going to

#漿＝浆 jiāng；奖,桨,蒋 jiǎng；酱,将 jiàng；锵 qiāng.

* A piece of pork being put on a chopping block. PLC.　[鼎 dǐng, 刀 dāo, 肉 ròu, 寸 cùn, 片 piàn]

用手将肉置在几俎上。

zhě

者

— person who does (something)；functions like "-er"；a surname

#赭,锗 zhě；躇 chú；储,楮 chǔ；都 dōu；睹,堵,赌 dǔ；都,嘟 dū；奢 shē；署,暑,曙,薯 shǔ；屠 tú；绪 xù；猪,诸,楮,潴,橥 zhū；渚,煮 zhǔ；著,箸 zhù.

* Shows food being put into a pot. The kind of food is not clear. The lower 日 rì derives from the drawing of the pot. PLC, 煮 zhǔ: to boil, cook；with a lower fire-radical.　[隹 zhuī: bird, 火 huǒ: fire]

者是煮的本字,象将食物投放到锅中形。

125

xiāng
香

甲骨  篆文

— fragrant; appetizing; popular; perfume or spice; incense

馥 fù: fragrance; 馨 xīn: strong and pervasive fragrance.

* Shows rice 禾 **hé**: rice (or 来 **lái**: wheat in ancient pictographs) being put into a pot.　[者 zhě]
将禾放入锅内。

jù
具
甲骨  金文 古文 篆文

— implement, utensil; to provide; to possess; ability; a unit of things

俱, 颶, (惧＝懼)jù.

* Hands holding up a cooking vessel.
[鼎 dǐng, 共 gòng]
象双手持鼎(或贝)之形。

dēng
登
甲骨 金文  古文 篆文

— to ascend; to record

燈＝灯, 噔, 蹬 dēng; 凳, 鄧＝邓, 瞪, 澄, 嶝, 磴, 镫 dèng; 橙, 澄 chéng; 證＝证 zhèng.

* The upper two footprints in the ancient forms of 登 **dēng** represented moving forward or presenting. Thus, 登 **dēng** showed two hands holding a *dou*-bowl to present an offering to the gods or their ancestors. Later, the hands were omitted. 豆 **dòu** is also a phonetic element.　[共 gòng, 止 zhǐ, 豆 dòu]
登表示(双手)捧豆升阶以敬神。

zào
皂
甲骨 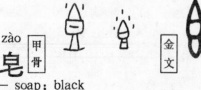 金文 篆文

— soap; black

簋 guǐ; 唣 zào; 即 jí; 既 jì; 食 shí.

* A bowl containing food. PLC, 簋 **guǐ**: a round-mouthed food vessel with two or four loop handles.
[豆 dòu, 皿 mǐn]
象碗(豆)中有饭之形。

jí
即 甲骨

— to approach, reach, be near; to undertake; at present; prompted by the occasion
唧 jī；鯽 jì；節＝节 jié；楖 zhì；卿 qīng.

* A man preparing for dinner. PLC.
[皂 zào，卩 jié]
象人就食之形。

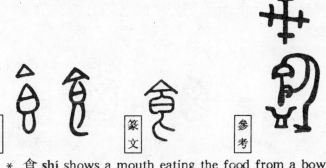

shí
食 甲骨

— to eat；food, meal；feed；edible；eclipse

* 食 shí shows a mouth eating the food from a bowl. The top "A" is a drawing of the open mouth, and the dots in the ancient pictographs represent saliva. This character is a radical for food or eating.
[饣 as radical，皂 zào]
象人张嘴吃饭之形。

shù
术 甲骨

— archaic form of 秫 shú
術＝术：skill, technique, 述 shù；秫 shú；怵 chù；术 zhú.

* Sticky food adhering to a hand. PLC, 秫 shú：glutinous sorghum. [又 yòu，禾 hé]
象粘(nián)食粘(zhān)手之形。

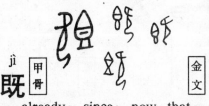

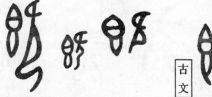

jì
既 甲骨

— already；since；now that；both...(and)...
暨 jì；溉，概 gài；慨 kǎi.

* Depicts a man having enjoyed his dinner. PLC.
[皂 zào，即 jí]
象人吃完饭调头欲走之形。

127

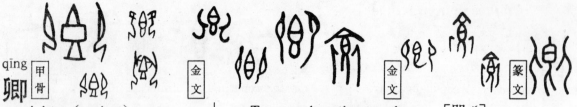

qīng
卿
[甲骨] [金文] [金文] [篆文]

— minister (ancient)

饗＝饟 xiǎng：to provide dinner for，entertain；鄉＝乡 xiāng.

* Two people eating together.   ［即 jí］

象两人在一起吃饭之形。卿即饟，二字同源。

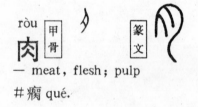

lǔ
鹵＝卤
[金文] [篆文]

— bittern

* A bag containing salt. The four dots are grains of salt. It is a radical for some characters. PLC，鹽＝盐 yán：salt；鹽＝监 jiān is a phonetic element.

象盐袋之形。

ròu
肉
[甲骨] [篆文]

— meat，flesh；pulp
癯 qué.

* 肉 ròu is usually supposed to be a drawing of a piece of meat. However，it may derive from the mouth and fangs of a carnivorous animal such as 能 néng：pictograph of a bear. 肉 ròu is a radical，written as 月 yuè，referring to the human's body.

象肉块形。

yǒu
有
[甲骨] [金文] [篆文]

— to have，possess；to exist
肴 yáo；淆 xiáo；铕 yǒu；侑，宥，圃，有 yòu；贿 huì.

* A hand holding a piece of meat. The top 又 yòu is also a phonetic element.   ［又 yòu，肉 ròu，牛 niú］

象手持一块肉形。

5.3 Clothes and Ornament 衣饰

biǎo
表 [古文]  [篆文]

— surface, outside; exterior; to show, to express; list
#褾，婊，錶＝表 biǎo.

* A fur coat with the pelt on the outside.
[毛 máo：hair；fur，衣 yī：clothes]
表从衣从毛。古人以兽皮为衣，皮里毛外。

qiú
求 [甲骨]  [金文] 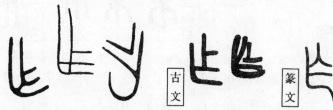 [古文] [篆文]

— to request; to try; demand
#俅，逑，球，赇，裘 qiú；救 jiù.

* A fur coat. 又 **yòu** is a phonetic element. Later, the "fur coat" component was simplified as four dots. PLC，裘 **qiú**：fur coat.　[衣 yī，表 biǎo，又 yòu]
求为裘字之省，表示毛皮大衣。

zhà
乍 [甲骨]  [金文] [古文] [篆文]

— for the first time; abruptly
#咋，炸，痄，蚱，诈，榨，柞 zhà；砟 zhǎ；咋 zǎ；怎 zěn；窄 zhǎi；作 zuō；作，昨，笮 zuó；作，祚，柞，酢，胙，阼 zuò.

* Stitching the neckband of an ancient garment. PLC，作 **zuò**：to make.　[衣 yī]
乍表示缝制衣领。一说乍是用耒翻土耕作。

▶ 蓑笠。
笠 lì

shuāi
衰 [篆文]

— to decline, wane
#蓑 suō.

* A straw raincoat. PLC，蓑 **suō**：straw or palm-bark raincoat.　[衣 yī，草 cǎo]
人穿蓑衣形。

suō
蓑

jīn 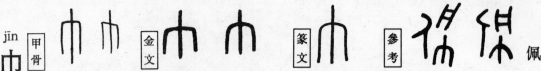 佩

巾

— a piece of cloth (as used for a towel, scarf, kerchief, etc.)

佩 pèi: to wear, admire.

* A scarf. It is a radical for cloth.

象佩巾之形。

bù

布

— cloth; to arrange

怖 bù.

* A pictophone. The phonetic element 父 **fù** incorrectly transformed into 又 **yòu** in the modern 布 **bù**.　〔父 fù or 又 yòu, 巾 jīn〕

形声字。声符"父"后被"又"所替代。

bó

帛

— silks

锦 jǐn; 棉,绵 mián.

* A pictophone.　〔白 bái, 巾 jīn〕

形声字,从巾白声。

bì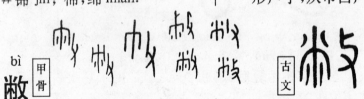

敝

— worn-out, shabby (written); my

幣=币, 蔽 bì; 憋,鳖 biē; 蹩 bié; 撇, 瞥 piē; 撇 piě; 弊, 獘= 斃 bì.

* A hand holding a duster to brush dust (the four dots) off a piece of ragged clothing.　〔巾 jīn, 父 fù〕

手持木棍掸去巾上的尘土。

mào

冒

— to send out; to risk; rashly; a surname

帽，瑁 mào.

* A person wearing a headgear with that leaves the eye, 目 mù, uncovered. PLC, 帽 mào：hat; with a radical 巾 jīn. [目 mù, 冑 zhòu]

象人头上戴有帽子，眼睛露在外面。

cān

参＝参 [金文]

— to pay one's respects to (a superior, etc.); to take part in

骖 cān；惨 cǎn；掺 chān；参 shēn；渗 shèn；参 cēn.

* A person wearing a beautiful head ornaments or perhaps a man standing under a certain constellation. [星 xīng, 大 dà, 彡 shān and 人参 rénshēn：ginseng]

象头上有装饰的人形。后又加三，分化出表示数目之叁。

xiǎn

顯＝显 [金文]

— to show, display; apparent, obvious, noticeable

濕＝湿 shī；隰 xí.

* Hair arranged in braids. [页 yiè, 丝 sī]

象人头上的发辫。

ruò

若 [甲骨]

— like, seem, as if; if

偌，篛 ruò；匿 nì；喏，诺，锘 nuò；若，惹 rě.

* Shows a person putting his hair in order with his hands. PLC. [毛 máo，又 yòu，卩 jié]

象人双手理顺头发形。

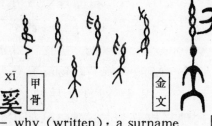

xī

奚 [甲骨] [金文] [篆文]

— why (written); a surname

溪，蹊，蹊 xī；鷄＝鸡 jī；蹊 qī.

* A person wearing a queue or a pigtail. PLC. [爪 zhǎo，大 dà，显 xiǎn]

象人手编辫子。古代奚是一个辫发的族称。

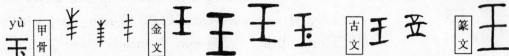

— jade;（of a woman）beautiful

宝＝寶 bǎo：treasure；珏 jué：two joined pieces of jade.

[汉]许慎《说文解字》玉字条。
JADE（*from Xu, Shen*）.

* A string of jade beads. The dot was a late addition in order to distinguish 玉 **yù** from 王 **wáng**.

The manufacture of jade object began in China's Neolithic Period. Jade is rather loosely understood by the Chinese to include both nephrite and jadeite as well as other hard stones. More important than such distinctions are the objects carved from those hard stones. These objects are intrinsically valuable and metaphorically equated with human virtues because of their hardness, durability, rarity, and beauty.

[王 as radical]

象贯穿起来的一串玉饰。

玉,石之美者。中国的制玉历史始于新石器时代。玉石艺术是中国文化的一个组成部分,它是中国人对石器时代先民制造石器工具的一种升华。玉石的品种众多,其稀有程度也有非常大的差异,因此中国人对玉石没有严格的定义。对中国人来讲更为重要的是玉石的雕刻,以及通过陈设和佩戴玉制品所反映出的人的品质和精神。

古代中国人所称的玉,用近代矿物学来分类,可分为两大类:一是软玉(nephrite);一类是硬玉(jadeite),也就是翡翠。一般所说的玉都属闪石类(amphibole group),颜色白的和透闪石(tremolite)相近,颜色绿的和阳起石(actinolite)相近。透闪石的理想成分为 $Ca_2Mg_5Si_8O_{22}(OH)_2$ 阳起石的理想成分为 $Ca_2(Mg, Fe^{2+})_5Si_8O_{22}(OH)_2$,均属单斜晶系。翡翠今属辉石类(pyroxene group),一般又分为两种:红的是翡,绿的是翠。翡是含锰的青辉石(violan),色红紫带青,往往和翠(jadeite)共生,而且也是同属,所以合称翡翠。翡翠的理想成分为 $NaAlSi_2O_6$,属单斜晶系,主要产于缅甸。

132

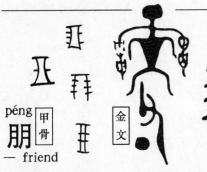

péng 甲骨 金文
朋
— friend
棚,硼,鹏 péng；崩,绷,嘣 bēng；绷,蹦 bèng.

* A string of cowry shells. Cowry shell was used as both money and jewelry in early Chinese civilization. The form of this element 月 **yuè** derives from 贝 **bèi**: cowry. PLC.

以贝为饰。北京周口店山顶洞人遗址发现有顶部磨出洞的贝。

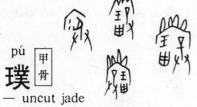

pú 甲骨
璞
— uncut jade
醭 bú；扑=扑,噗 pū；僕=仆,镤 pú；樸=朴,蹼 pǔ.

* The ancient form of 璞 **pú** shows a jade hunter on a mountain digging jade and putting it in his basket.
[玉 yù, 父 fù, 山 shān]
象人在山上采集玉石。

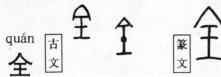

quán 古文 篆文
全
— to keep intact; to complete; whole, entire; entirely; a surname
荃,痊,诠,铨,醛,筌 quán；拴,栓 shuān.

* A man placed over a piece of jade, or with jade placed between his legs, indicating his ownership of the piece. PLC. [大 dà, 玉 yù]
象人胯下有玉形。

nòng 甲骨 金文
弄
— to do; to play; to play with

* Admiring a jade piece held in one's hands.
[玉 yù, 又 yòu or 共 gòng]
双手赏玩玉形。

133

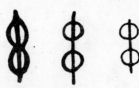

chuàn
串 [金文]

— string; to string together

＃患 huàn;（窜＝竄 cuàn）.

* A string of two (jade) beads.
象串起来的两个玉珠之形。

 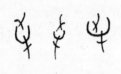

guài
夬 [甲骨] [篆文]

— a term in *The Book of Changes*
（《易经》）

＃决，抉，诀，觖 jué；快，筷，
（块＝塊）kuài；袂 mèi；缺，炔
quē.

* The two hands holding a 玦 **jué**：a penannular jade ring. PLC, 玦 **jué**.
象人双手持玦之形。玦为环状而有缺口的玉璧。

huáng
黄 [甲骨] [金文] [古文] [篆文]

— yellow, sallow; decadent,
obscene, pornographic

＃蟥，璜，磺，簧 huáng；横
héng；横 hèng.

* A person wearing a jade pendant and cheerfully opening his mouth upward. PLC, 璜 **huáng**：semi-annular jade pendant.　　[大 dà]
象人佩戴环形玉饰。

dài
带＝帶 [金文] [篆文]

— belt, band; take, to bring; to
lead

＃滞 zhì.

* A belt buckle with tassels.　　[巾 jīn]
象衣服钩带相连之形。带字上部为钩带的变形，
下面两"巾"相叠，为装饰用下垂的须子。

5.4　Habitation　居住

汉瓦当。

hù
户 [甲骨] [金文] [古文] [篆文]

— family；(bank) account
#（滬＝沪，護＝护），戽，扈 hù；妒 dù；雇 gù.

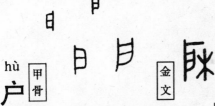

mén
門＝门 [甲骨]

— door；gate；way to do sth；
knack；a surname
#扪,钔 mén；们 men；闷 mēn；
闷,焖 mèn；闩 shuān：bolt,
latch.

* A door.
一扇门形。

關

* Double doors or a gate. It is a radical. 　[户 hù]
象门形。

kāi
開＝开 [古文] [篆文]

— to open；to make a opening；
to come loose；to start, operate
#锎 kāi.

* Two hands removing the large bolt from a gate.
[闩 shuān：bolt, 又 yòu or 共 gòng]
象双手打开门闩形。

qǐ
啓＝启 [甲骨] [金文] [古文] [篆文]

— to open；to start, initiate
#綮 qìng；肇 zhào.

* A hand opening a door. 　[户 hù, 口 kǒu, 又 yòu, 父 fù]
启表示用手开启门户。

135

婦

zhǒu 帚 甲骨 金文 篆文 参考

— broom

婦＝妇 fù：married woman；
掃 ＝扫 sǎo：to sweep；sào：
broom.

* A broom.
象扫帚之形。

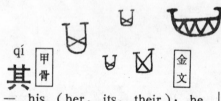

sào 埽 甲骨 篆文 参考

— to throw away, discard；to
abandon (archaic)

浸 jìn；侵 qīn；寝 qǐn：to
sleep (to sweep the bed off with
the broom).

* A hand holding a broom. The radical 土 **tǔ**：dust,
is a later addition. [帚 zhǒu，又 yòu]

qí 其 甲骨 金文 古文 篆文

— his (her, its, their)；he
(she, it, they)；that；such

其,淇,骐,琪,棋,祺,蜞,綦,
麒 qí；期,欺 qī；箕,基 jī.

* A bin or dustpan；the lower element is phonetic.
PLC，箕 **jī**：dustpan, with a bamboo radical. [基 jī]
象簸箕之形。

rǎn 冉 甲骨 金文 篆文

— slowly

髯,蚺 rán；苒 rǎn.

* A bamboo crate. PLC.
象竹编器形。

xūn
熏
— to smoke, fumigate
薰: sweetgrass, fragrance, 曛, 醺 xūn; 熏 xùn.

＊ A bunch of savory being burnt for incense.
[黑 hēi: black, 火 huǒ: fire]
象一束点燃的香草。

jī
几 篆文
— a small table
肌 jī; 麂 jǐ.

＊ A small table. [几 jǐ]
象小桌之形。

pán
爿 甲骨 篆文
— a flat, thin piece

＊ A wooden bed. It is a radical referring to plank-like object. PLC. [片 piàn]
象床几形,床形竖立是由于刻写方便。

◀ 榻·[宋]槐荫消夏图。

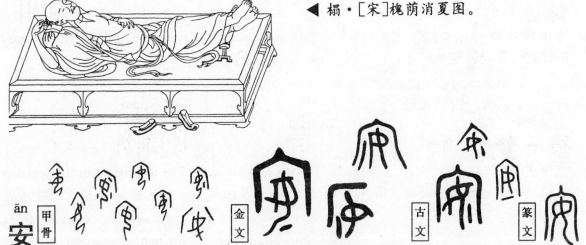

ān
安 甲骨 金文 古文 篆文
— safe; settled, calm; to install; a surname
按, 桉, 氨, 鞍 ān; 铵 ǎn; 按, 案, 胺 àn; 黶 yǎn; 晏, 宴 yàn.

＊ Shows a woman kneeling in a room. The rules of decency required that proper women spent most of their lives sequestered in the home.
[六 liù or 宀 mián, 女 nǚ]
女子在房中,表示安详悠闲。

yīn 因

甲骨

金文 古文 篆文

— cause, reason; because of; to follow (written); in accordance with

茵, 姻, 氤, 铟 yīn; 恩, 葱 ēn; 咽, 烟, 胭 yān; 咽 yàn, yè.

* A woven mat. The character 大 dà in 因 yīn derives from the woven pattern. PLC, 茵 yīn: mattress; with a grass-radical.

象席形。

sù 宿
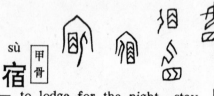
甲骨

金文 古文 篆文

— to lodge for the night, stay over night; long-standing, veteran (written); a surname

缩 suō; 宿 xiǔ: one night; 宿 xiù; 蓿 xu.

* A man sleeping in a room. The element 百 bǎi derives from the drawing of a mat.

[六 liù, 人 rén, 因 yīn]

象人在屋内坐卧于席上。

xiū 休

甲骨

金文 古文 篆文

— to rest; to stop

咻, 庥, 貅, 鸺, 鬃 xiū.

* A person resting against a tree.   [人 rén, 木 mù]

象人倚树休息之形。

mèng 夢＝梦
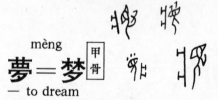
甲骨

古文 篆文

— to dream

薨 hōng; 甍, 瞢 méng; 懵 měng.

* A man and his bed. The bed indicates the location where dreams occur. The man is pointing to his eye; perhaps he is giving a glowing account of the tempting or tormenting dream he just had. The upper part, the dreamer's dancing eyebrow, may also derive from 眉 méi: eyebrow, as a phonetic element, and the bottom 夕 xī: night, is a meaning element added later.

[爿 pán, 眉 méi, 夕 xī]

象人在夜里做梦。

138

jiān 甲骨 金文 古文 篆文

监 = 监

— to supervise; prison

\# 监，艦 = 舰，鑒 = 鉴，槛 jiàn；
槛 kǎn；蓝，篮，褴 lán；滥 làn；
鹽 = 盐 yán.

* A man using a water-filled vessel as a mirror. PLC, 鑒 = 鉴 **jiàn**：mirror；with a metal-radical. Ancient mirrors were made of bronze.

［见 jiàn，臣 chén，皿 mǐn，金 jīn］
象人俯身低头向盘中水面照看状。

 篆文 参考

yíng
甲骨

盈

— to be full of, be filled with;
have a surplus of

\# 楹 yíng.

* Portrays a man standing in a big vessel to take a bath. ［人 rén，又 yòu or 止 zhǐ，皿 mǐn］
象人在盆中洗澡形。

niào 甲骨 金文

尿

— urine; to urinate

\# 疹，畛，诊，轸 zhěn；珍
zhēn；趁 chèn；殄 tiǎn；饕 tiè.

* Shows a person passing water. PLC.
［人 rén，尸 shī，水 shuǐ，㐱 zhěn：archaic character］
象人小解形。

 篆文

chuáng
甲骨

爿

— archaic character

* A diaphoretic patient lying on a bed. It is a radical for characters related to disease. ［爿 pán，人 rén］
象病人躺在床上发汗之形。

wèi
尉
— an officer, a military rank
#蔚,慰 wèi；熨 yùn.

* Shows a patient being cauterized by burning moxa, moxibustion. PLC, 熨 **yùn**：to iron（clothes）；with another "fire", 火 **huǒ**, as a lower radical.
［尸 shī, 父 fù or 寸 cùn, 火 huǒ］
尉字可能反映了古代的艾灸疗法。

yīn
殷
— name of dynasty；thriving

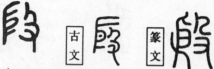

* A patient undergoing acupuncture treatment. PLC.
［身 shēn, 父 fù or 殳 shū］
象病人接受砭针治疗。

5.5   Interrelationship   交往

huà
化
— to change；culture；chemistry
#花, 化 huā；讹 é；货 huò：commodity；靴 xuē：boots.

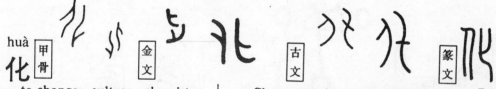

* Shows people coming and going.   ［人 rén］
象一正一倒两人形,表示人们来往变化交易的意思。

dé
旱
— the ancient form of 得 dé：to get
#得,锝 dé；得 děi.

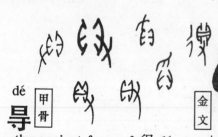

* A hand holding a cowry shell, which was used as money. 且 **dàn** is a simplified form of 贝 **bèi**.
［贝 bèi, 又 yòu or 寸 cùn］
象手得贝形。

măi

買＝买

— to buy, purchase

#賣＝卖 mài：to sell；觌 dí；
窦，读 dòu；渎，犊，牍，读，黩
dú；赎 shú：to redeem；续 xù.

* A cowry shell being dredged up with a net.

[网 wăng，贝 bèi]

买表示网获宝贝之形。

guàn

貫＝贯

— a string of 1000 copper coin；
pass through，pierce；a surname
#惯，掼 guàn；實＝实 shí.

* String of cowry shells.　　[贝 bèi]

象串起的两个贝形。

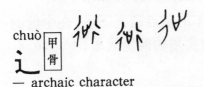

xíng

行

— to go；to travel；to do；
behaviour，conduct；all right
#行，绗 háng；珩，衡，桁 héng.

* Diagram of a crossroad. Both 行 **xíng** and the left-hand part 彳 **chì** are radicals implying motion.

象十字道路之形。

chuò

辶

— archaic character

* A combination of 彳 **chì** and 止 **zhĭ**：footprint. It is a radical.　　[行 xíng，止 zhĭ]

彳与止的结合。

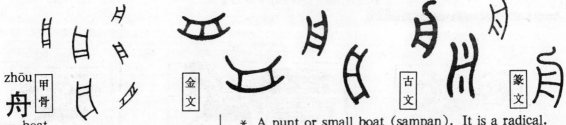

zhōu

舟

— boat

* A punt or small boat (sampan). It is a radical.

象舟船形。

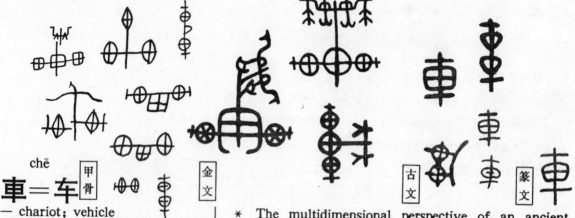

yōu
攸
— passing to, toward; past
悠 yōu；修 xiū；倏 shū；條
=条 tiáo；绦 táo；涤 dí.

* Shows a man rowing with an oar.［人 rén，父 fù］
象人持桨划水形，表示行水悠远。

chē
車＝车
— chariot；vehicle
轟＝轰 hōng；擊＝击 jī；车
jū；库 kù；阵 zhèn.

* The multidimensional perspective of an ancient chariot with spokes, shaft and yokes. In the modern version, 车 chē is a top view of the chariot's box with an axle and two wheels (two strokes on the axle). In Shang and Zhou Dynasties, the chariot was a symbol of the might of both kings and lords. It was also used as a practical weapon in warfare. See below.

古文字车源于古代车的散点透视图形。在中国的商周时代，车是指一种实用的两轮战车。

Rubbing of bricks, the Han Dynasty.
汉代画像砖。

厄 è [金文]
— adversity

#扼,苊,呃,轭 è.

* The yoke of a chariot. PLC, 轭 è：yoke；with a chariot-radical.

[车 chē, 两 liǎng, 扼 è：to grip, clutch]

象轭形。

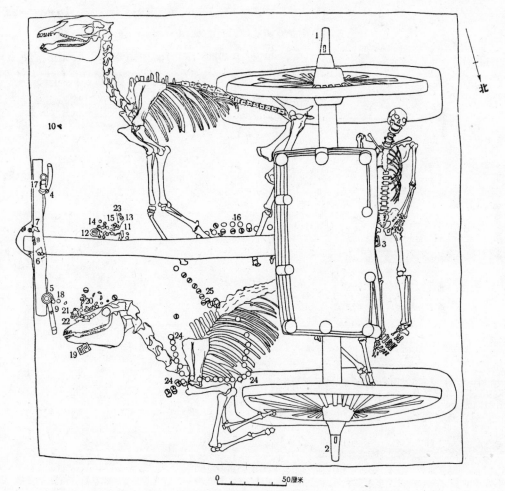

北

图一 车马坑平面图

1、2.軎 3.踵饰 4、5.轭饰 6、7.兽面形衡饰 9、10.铜鼻 11、19.铜镳 12、21.特大铜泡
13、20.小兽面形铜饰 14.镞形铜饰(另一件包括在 22 内) 8、15—18、22—25.铜泡

Plan of a late Shang dynasty chariot burial excavated at Xiaomintun, Anyang.

安阳孝民屯商代车马坑平面图(采自《考古》1972/4, p. 25)。

liǎng

两＝两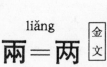

一 two; *liang*, a unit of weight (50 gram)

＃俩, 魉 liǎng; 辆 liàng; 俩 liǎ.

* Drawing of the shaft, cross bar and two yokes of a chariot. The top horizontal stroke is a later addition, it has a function of beautification. Two horses were yoked to the chariot. The shaft and cross bar of a chariot could be used as a pair of scales by the ancient merchants in their trades; so 两 **liǎng** was also borrowed to represent a unit of weight.

[辆 liàng: a classifier for vehicles, 车 chē, 厄 è]

　　两字源于车辕与车衡的象形,中间的"从"表示车衡上的两个轭。

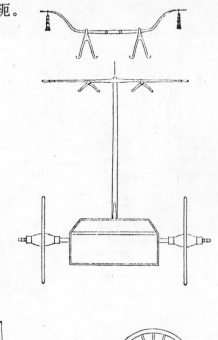

Chariot

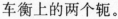

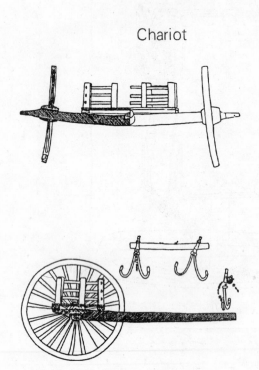

Shang Dynasty

West Zhou Dynasty

The yokes of chariots.

车衡。

Chapter 6

THE EMERGENCE OF WAR 战争的出现

6.1   Weaponry and the Military   兵器与军事力量

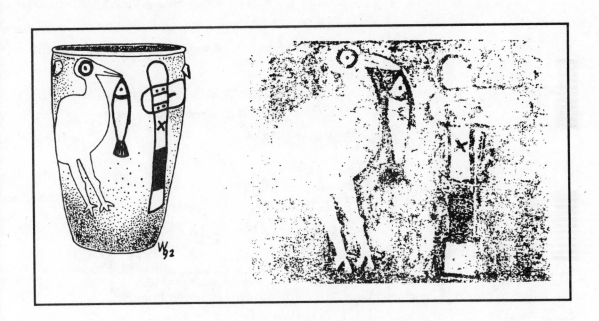

A Neolithic clay vessel with the design of a stork holding a fish in its mouth. Both the stork and the fish are totems, symbols for two clans. The stone ax on the design alludes that this vessel was a victory souvenir for the winner, the stork-clan, fighting against the fish-clan.

彩陶缸·鹳衔鲢鱼石斧。河南临汝出土,仰韶文化庙底沟型。

这件彩绘陶缸是用来装殓某个部落首长的。画面高三十七厘米,宽四十四厘米,由棕白两色构成。彩画中的白鹳与鲢鱼含有部落图腾的意味。捆扎在木棍上的石斧和白鹳衔鲢鱼的造形,记录了白鹳氏族战胜鲢鱼氏族的历史事件。

6. 1. 1—Armory　军械库

gē
甲骨　金文

戈

— dagger-ax; a surname

（劃＝划 huá：to scratch）;
戟 jǐ: halberd; 戕: to kill, 戗:
to clash　qiāng; 找 zhǎo: to
look for.

* A bronze dagger-ax or *ge*-halberd with a long shaft
and tang. The upper dot of this character derives from
the upper curved end of the shaft instead of the
halberd's spike. The stroke on the shaft's butt indicates
the finial. The *Ge* was a principal weapon of the Shang
and Zhou Dynasties as well as an important element in
this chapter.

　　戈是一种古代格斗兵器。戈的使用与发展历经
商周两代,直到公元前三世纪,它是上古时期一种
主要的实战兵器。

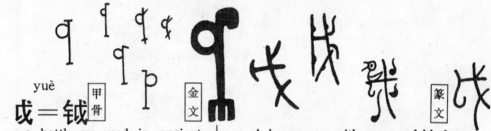

yuè
甲骨　金文

戉＝钺

— a battle-ax used in ancient
China

越 yuè.

* A bronze ax with a curved blade.
是一种用于劈砍格斗的斧形兵器。

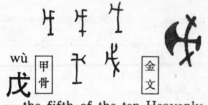

wù
甲骨　金文

戊

— the fifth of the ten Heavenly
Stems

茂 mào.

* A bronze ax. This character was later borrowed to
represent one element of the decimal cycle.
［钺 yuè，戌 xū］
　　一种古代平刃战斧。

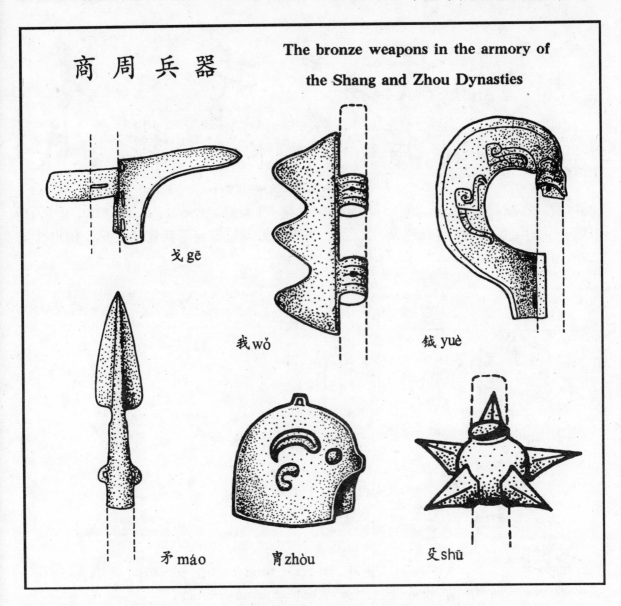

商周兵器

The bronze weapons in the armory of the Shang and Zhou Dynasties

戈 gē

我 wǒ

钺 yuè

矛 máo

胄 zhòu

殳 shū

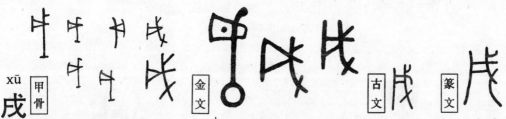

xū

戌 甲骨 金文 古文 篆文

— the eleventh of the twelve Earthly Branches

\# 威 wēi；滅 = 灭 miè：to kill, extinguish.

* Drawing of a battle-ax with a long shaft. PLC.

［戌 wù，戌 shù，戎 róng］

战斧象形。

147

wǒ 甲骨 金文 古文 篆文 参考
我
— I, myself
俄，哦，娥，蛾，鹅，莪，峨 é；
饿 è；哦 ó，ò；硪 wò；義 = 义
yì.

* A saw-ax with a wave-like or zigzag blade and a tubular socket attaching it to the shaft. PLC. [戈 gē]
一种古代刃部呈锯齿形兵器的象形。假借作第一人称代词。

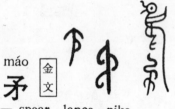

máo 金文 篆文
矛
— spear, lance, pike
茅，蝥 máo；袤，瞀，懋 mào.

* Sketch of a tasselled bronze lance.
格斗用长柄刺兵器。

shū 金文 篆文
殳
— mace
股 gǔ；没 méi；没，殁 mò；
芟 shān；设 shè；投，骰 tóu；
役，疫 yì.

* Shows a hand holding a mace — a club with a heavy head of stone or bronze.
[父 fù，攴 pū：to beat lightly]
手持殳形。（攴从又卜声。）

dùn 甲骨 金文 篆文 参考
盾

— shield

遁 dùn；循 xún.

* Shows a man holding an oval shield. The small cross indicates the handle of the shield. In the Shang and Zhou Dynasties, most shields were made of animal skin strengthened by a coat of lacquer.

人手持盾牌形。

zhòu 金文

冑

— helmet; descendants

* A bronze helmet with a *panache*, a plume or tuft of feathers, on top. The lower 月 yuè was incorrectly derived from 目 mù：eye.　[冒 mào]

象人头戴头盔,眼睛露在外面的样子。

jiè 甲骨　金文　古文　篆文

介

— armor, shell; to be between; to take seriously

价,芥,疥,界,骱 jiè；芥 gài；

(價＝价 jià；階＝阶 jiē).

* Shows a soldier girding on his armor.　[人 rén]

人身着片状盔甲形。

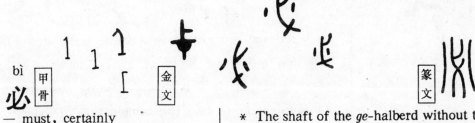

bì 甲骨　金文　篆文

必

— must, certainly

秘,铋,泌,毖 bì；密,嘧,蜜,泌,秘,谧 mì；瑟 sè.

* The shaft of the *ge*-halberd without the blade. PLC, 柲 bì：shaft of ancient weapons. The two dots on the sides are either later additions for decoration's sake, or an ancient phonetic element 八 bā.　[戈 gē]

象戈矛等兵器的柄形。

6. 1. 2—Archery   弓箭术

Rock Painting • Bow man

岩画   弓箭手

Rock Painting (*after Gai* (1) *fig.* 49).

gōng 甲骨 金文 古文 篆文 参考

— bow; bent, crooked

躬 gōng：to bow；窮＝穷，
穹 qióng；發＝发 fā：to send
out.

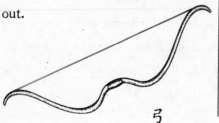

弓

* A reflexed composite bow (before being strung).
Reflexion places the limbs of a bow under greater
tension when the bow is strung, storing more power
than straight bows do. The combination of extended
draw length and short limbs enables the composite bow
to shoot an arrow faster and farther than can a wooden
straight bow of equal draw weight (see below).

复合回复弓的象形。

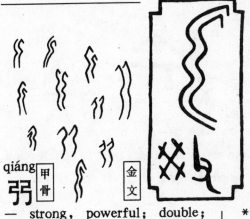

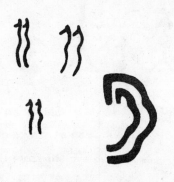

qiáng
弱 甲骨 金文

— strong, powerful; double;
multiple
弼 bì: to assist; 弱 ruò:
weak, feeble; 粥 zhōu; 鬻 yù;
强 qiáng: strong.

* Ancient China's bowmakers used adhesives derived from hide and fish's swim bladders to glue animal sinew to the backs of their bows. They also painted thick layers of lacquer on the bow backs. Both the sinew and the lacquer have high tensile strength. Other materials such as horn were sometimes glued to the bellies of wood or bamboo reflexed bows to reinforce the compressive loads. [弓 gōng]

中国古代的工匠用把动物筋腱粘在弓背上，或在弓背上涂上多层大漆的方法来制造强背复合弓。

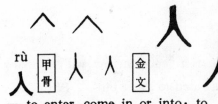

rù
入 甲骨 入 入 金文 入 古文 入 篆文 入

— to enter, come in or into; to
take in
氽 cūan.

* Represents an arrowhead. PLC.
入表示箭头。

▶ **Bone arrowheads from Banpo, the Neolithic** (*after Lindqvist*).

骨制箭头，半坡遗址出土。

shǐ 矢 [甲骨] [金文] [古文] [篆文]

— arrow; to vow, swear

知 zhī.

* Shows an arrow with its arrowhead and nock. The short stroke on the arrow shaft was used to differentiate 矢 **shǐ** from the ancient forms of 大 **dà** and 交 **jiāo**.

象箭形。

yín 寅 [甲骨] [金文] [古文] [篆文]

— the third of the twelve Earthly Branches

螾 yín; 演 yǎn.

* 寅 **yín** and 矢 **shǐ**: arrow are cognate characters. When 寅 **yín** was borrowed to use in the duodecimal cycle, a square symbol was added on the shaft.

寅矢同源分化。

yí 夷 [金文] [古文] [篆文]

— smooth, safe; to raze; to exterminate

姨, 痍, 胰, 咦 yí.

* Drawing shows a retrievable arrow with a string attached to it . It was used to shoot birds . PLC.

[矢 **shǐ**, 弋 **yì**: a retrievable arrow with a string attached to it]

象古代射鸟用的一种拴有丝绳便于回收的箭。

Detail of a bronze jar from the Zhou period. See the whole design on page 60.

弋射。

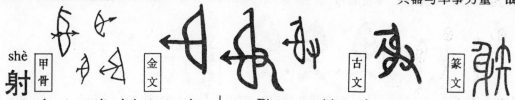

shè
射 甲骨 金文 古文 篆文

— to shoot, emit, inject; to aim at

麝 shè; 榭, 谢 xiè.

* Picture writings show an arrow being shot. Later, the bow and arrow were replaced with the element 身 shēn. [弓 gōng, 又 yòu or 寸 cùn]

手引弓箭形。后来弓与箭的组合用"身"代替了。

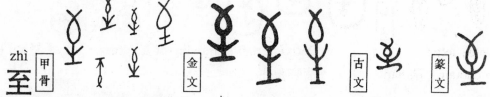

zhì
至 甲骨 金文 古文 篆文

—to come to, reach, attain; so far, to the extent

桎, 致, 窒, 蛭, 轾, 郅, 膣 zhì; 侄, 侄 zhí; 室 shì; 到, 倒 dào; 倒 dǎo.

* Shows an arrow hitting its target, or the ground. [矢 shǐ.]

象矢中靶或矢远来落地之形。

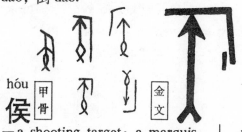

hóu
侯 甲骨 金文 古文 篆文

—a shooting target; a marquis, a rank of nobility; a surname

喉, 猴, 篌, 瘊 hóu; 候 hòu.

* Shows an arrow flying to a shooting target. Later, the form of "target" is changed, a man-radical being substituted for the left side. [矢 shǐ, 厂 hàn]

象矢射侯(箭靶)之形。

bèi
備＝备 甲骨 金文 篆文

— to prepare, provide

惫 bèi.

* Shows arrows being placed in a frame. PLC.

象箭放置在器架中。

bì

畀

— to bestow

箅, 痹 bì; 鼻 bí.

* An arrow with a flat arrowhead. PLC.　[矢 shǐ]

象带有扁平箭头的箭形。

hán

函

— a case, shield; letter

涵 hán: to contain; 菡 hàn.

* Derives from a drawing of a quiver.　[矢 shǐ]

箭袋象形。

fú

弗

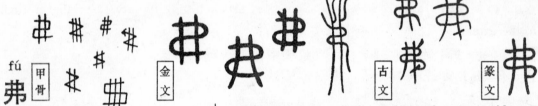

— not

佛, 怫, 拂, 绋, 氟 fú; 沸, 狒, 费, 镄 fèi; 佛 fó.

* Shows arrow shafts tied together to avoid warping. The "rope" element is written as a 弓 gōng. PLC.

将箭杆用绳捆在一起,不使其弯曲。

zhī

知

— to know, be aware of; knowledge

蜘 zhī; 智 zhì; 痴 chī; 踟 chí.

* A combination of 矢 **shǐ**: arrow and 口 **kǒu**: a symbol for the sound of a flying arrow. PLC.
[矢 shǐ, 口 kǒu]

从矢从口,表示射箭时的声音。

jí

疾

— disease, sickness; to abhor; fast, quick

蒺, 嫉 jí.

* A man being shot with an arrow.
[矢 shǐ, 大 dà, 疒 chuáng]

象矢射人形。也作疾病用。

6.1.3—Flag   旗帜

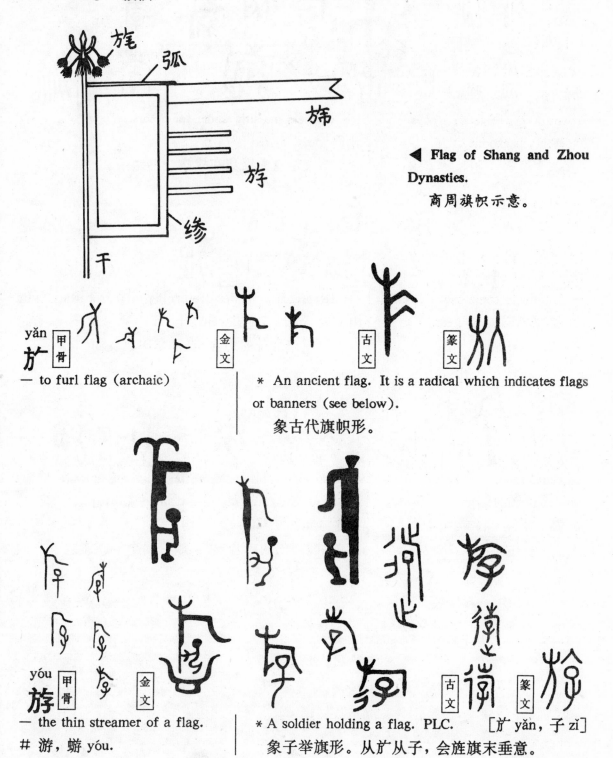

◀ **Flag of Shang and Zhou Dynasties.**

　　商周旗帜示意。

yǎn
扩 | 甲骨

— to furl flag (archaic)

* An ancient flag. It is a radical which indicates flags or banners (see below).

象古代旗帜形。

yóu
斿 | 甲骨 | 金文

— the thin streamer of a flag.

＃ 游，蝣 yóu.

* A soldier holding a flag. PLC.　　［扩 yǎn，子 zǐ］

象子举旗形。从扩从子，会旌旗末垂意。

155

旅 lǚ

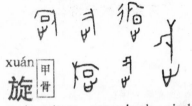

— to travel; brigade; troops

\# 膂 lǚ: backbone.

* Soldiers massing under the colors.

[疒 yǎn，人 rén]

旅表示众人聚集在战旗（疒）之下。

旋 xuán

— to return, come back; circle

\# 漩，璇 xuán; 旋 xuàn.

* Represents fighters returning （from battle） with flying colors.　[疒 yǎn，止 zhǐ]

旗帜与足趾的组合，表示举旗凯旋而归。

族 zú

— clan; race; a class of things with common features

\# 镞 zú; 簇 cù; 嗾 sǒu.

* A combination of a flag and an arrow, which indicates the gathering of a clan to do battle.

[疒 yǎn，矢 shǐ]

旗帜与矢的组合，表示族众集合于族旗之下。

6.2　Nation and Warfare　国家与战争

fù　甲骨　金文
父
— father

\# 父,釜,滏,斧 fǔ; 爸 bà;
pa; 爹 diē: father; 爺 = 爷 yé:
grandpa.

* A hand holding a celt or stone ax. PLC, 斧 fǔ: ax;
斤 jīn is a pictograph of a hatchet.　［又 yòu］
手持石斧形。

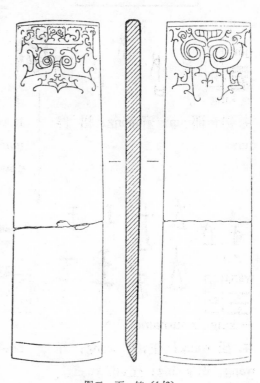

▶ A design on a ritual jade ax. Neolithic Period,
Longshan culture, late third millennium BC.
Excavated at *Rizhao Liangchengzhen* in
Shandong Province.

玉斧及其阴刻纹样。山东日照两城镇出土,龙山
文化。长 18.0,上宽 4.5、厚 0.85,下宽 4.9、厚
0.6(cm)。(采自《考古》1972/4. p.57, fig.2)。

图二　石　锛 (1/2)

gòng　甲骨　金文
共
— together; common; total; to
share

\# 供,恭 gōng; 拱 gǒng; 供
gòng; 哄,烘 hōng; 洪 hóng; 哄
hǒng; 哄 hòng.

* Two hands making an offering. PLC. 供 gòng: to
lay offerings.
［又 yòu, 廾 gǒng: action of two hands (古拱字)］
双手捧物进供。

157

◀ An inscription 共 gòng on a potsherd. Late Henan Longshan culture, 2000 BC. Excavated at *Dengfeng*, Henan Province. This inscription may indicate that this earthenware vessel was a peace offering.

陶文·共。

jūn
君
甲骨
— king

捃，郡 jùn；窘 jiǒng；裙，群 qún.

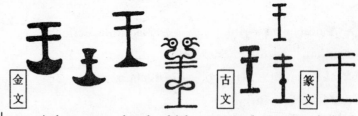

* A hand holding a stick or mace and issuing orders. It was thought that a monarch must possess both the mace and the magic flute—a symbol of persuasive power—to maintain his rule. [父 fù，口 kǒu：mouth]

手持权杖发号施令。

wáng
王
甲骨
— king; a surname

汪 wāng；往，枉 wǎng；旺 wàng；逛 guàng；狂，诳 kuáng.

* A bronze ax head which was used as a symbol of power.

象青铜战斧之形。

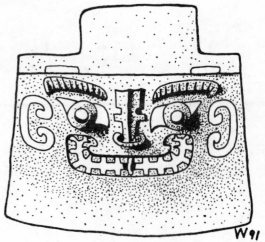

▶ A bronze ax head, Shang.
   商代青铜大钺。

huáng
皇
— emperor, sovereign
凰,隍,惶,徨,煌,蝗,篁,鳇 huáng.

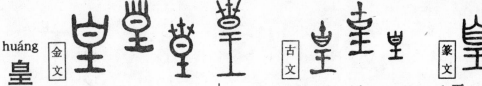

* A combination of a crown and 王 wáng: a symbol of power.　[王 wáng]
皇字上象皇冠,王为意符。

chén
臣
— official under a feudal ruler, subject; to acknowledge; allegiance to
卧 wò: to lie.

* Shows the eye of a bowing person.
[目 mù,见 jiàn,监 jiān]
臣表示人低头弯腰时侧目而视形。

huò
或
— or; probably; someone
惑 huò; 域,閾,蜮 yù; 國 = 国,掴,帼,馘 guó.

* This character is a combination of 戈 gē: dagger-ax and 口 kǒu: a symbol of a territory or city. The weapon is needed to protect the territory. PLC, 域 yù: territory; with a soil-radical; 國 = 国 guó: nation, country.　[戈 gē, 咸 xián]
或字中的"口"象城邑形,加戈表示守城。甲骨文或国一字。

wéi
韋 = 韦
— leather, a surname
帏,违,围: to enclose, 闱 wéi; 伟,苇,纬,玮,炜 wěi; 衛 = 卫 wèi; 韩 hán; 讳 huì; 韧 rèn.

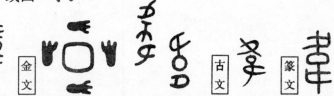

* Feet surrounding a square, a symbol which indicates the settlement or city, while the footprints represent a patrol. PLC, 衞 = 卫 wèi: to defend, protect; with the radical 行 xíng, implying action.　[止 zhǐ]
韦象城邑四周有足迹,表示巡逻护卫于城邑四周之意,为卫之初文。

zhèng 正 甲骨 金文 古文 篆文

— right, correct; proper, main; to rectify; just, exactly

怔,征,症,正 zhēng；证,政,症 zhèng；(惩＝懲 chěng).

* A footprint pointing to a city or settlement, intending to invade the city. Later, the small square, symbol for the city, was replaced by a single stroke. PLC, 征 **zhēng**：to invade, invasion; with a radical indicating movement.

[止 zhǐ, 足 zú, 彳 chì and see above]

正字从止,上面的一横源于城邑的象形。正是征的本字,表示征伐城邑。

fá 乏 金文 篆文

— exhausted; tired, weary; lack

砭 biān；贬 biǎn；泛 fàn；眨 zhǎ.

* Derives from the mirror image of 正 **zhèng**, see above. PLC.

乏字为正字之反。

zāi 戋 甲骨 金文 篆文

— calamity；wound (archaic)

载,哉 zāi；载 zǎi, zài；裁 cái；截 jié；戴 dài.

* An enemy's scalp on a *ge*-halberd to express defiance. The content of this character recalls the practice of scalping enemies also practiced by some North Amorican Indians during wartime. 才 **cái** was introduced into the character as a replacement for the scalp as well as for a phonetic element.

[毛 máo, 戈 gē, 才 cái, 灾 zāi：calamity]

将带有毛发的头皮系在戈上用来向敌方挑战。美洲印第安人也有剥取敌人头皮作为战利品的风俗。

bīng 兵 甲骨 金文 古文 篆文

160

— military；soldier

乒乓 pīngpāng；(賓＝宾,
傧，滨，缤，槟，镔 bīn；摈，
殡，膑，髌 bìn；梹 bīng).

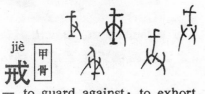

jiè 戒 甲骨

— to guard against；to exhort,
warn；to give up

诫 jiè：to admonish；械 xiè.

* Two hands holding an ax.　[斤 jīn，又 yòu]
双手持斧斤之形。

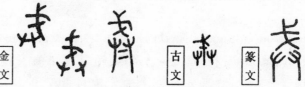

金文　古文　篆文

* Two hands holding a ge-halberd. [戈 gē，又 yòu]
双手持戈警戒之形。

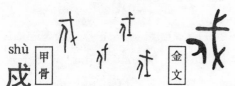

shù 戍 甲骨

— garrison；to guard a frontier

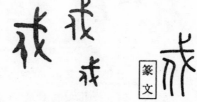

金文　篆文

* A combination of a man and a ge-halberd.
[人 rén，戈 gē]
象人立戈下之形，表示戍守。

hé 何 甲骨　金文　古文　篆文

— what, how, why (written)；
a surname

荷 hé, hè.

* A man carrying a ge-halberd. The small square is
used only to occupy the space under the halberd. 可 kě
is also a phonetic element. PLC, 荷 hè：to carry,
burden.　[人 rén，戈 gē，可 kě]
人荷戈形。

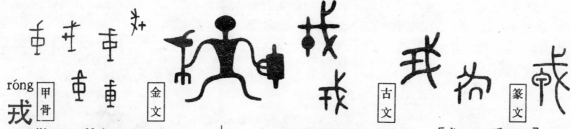

róng 戎 甲骨　金文　古文　篆文

— military affairs；a surname

绒 róng；贼 zéi.

* A ge-halberd and a shield.　[戈 gē，盾 dùn]
象兵士手持戈盾之形。

Fighting on a bridge. Rubbing of a frieze from the lintel of a tomb gate. Eastern Han Dynasty, Shandong Province. 胡汉两军桥上激战图。山东沂南画像石墓墓门门额拓片，东汉。(选自《中国大百科·考古学》，607页。)

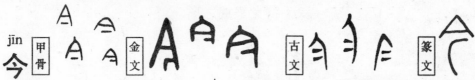

jīn
今
— today
衿 jīn；妗 jìn；岑，涔 cén；
钤，黔 qián；衾 qīn；芩，琴 qín；
贪 tān；陰＝阴，荫 yīn；吟 yín.

* An ancient bell. The outline of a bell is A-shaped, and the short stroke on the bottom of the pictograph indicates the tongue of the bell. PLC. See below.
今象古代的铃形。假借。

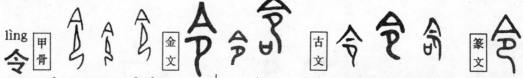

lìng
令
— to order, command；law
拎 līng；伶，苓，呤，图，铃，
玲，瓴，聆，蛉，羚，翎，零，龄
líng；令，嶺＝岭，领 lǐng；冷
lěng.

* A man-sitting or kneeling under a bell-symbol.
[今 jīn，卩 jié，命 mìng：order，铃 líng：bell]
人跪铃下受命之形。

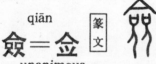

qiān
僉＝金
— unanimous
签 qiān；俭，捡，检，睑 jiǎn；
剑 jiàn；敛，脸，裣 liǎn；殓，潋
liàn；险 xiǎn；验 yàn.

* Shows people gathering to discuss military affairs after hearing the sound of a bell.
[今 jīn，令 lìn，口 kǒu，人 rén]
金表示众人听到铃声聚集之意。

wǔ
武

162

— military, martial; a surname
鹉 wǔ; 斌 bīn; 赋 fù.

* A ge-halberd and a footprint (a symbol of movement).   [戈 gē, 止 zhǐ]
武从戈从止,表示动武。

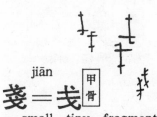

jiān 戔＝戈 [甲骨] [古文] [篆文] [参考]

— small, tiny, fragmentary
笺 jiān; 贱, 践: to trample, 溅, 饯 jiàn; 残 cán; 钱 qián; 浅 qiǎn; 线 xiàn; 盏 zhǎn; 栈 zhàn.

* Two ge-halberds in fighting position. PLC.
[戈 gē, 残 cán: to injure, ferocious]
从二戈相向,为残字的初文。

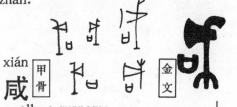 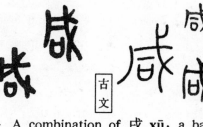

xián 咸 [甲骨] [金文] [古文] [篆文]

— all; a surname
鹹＝咸 xián; 感 gǎn; 喊 hǎn; 憾, 撼 hàn; 减, 碱 jiǎn; 缄 jiān; 箴 zhēn.

* A combination of 戌 xū: a battle-ax and 口 kǒu mouth. PLC.   [戌 xū, 口 kǒu, 喊 hǎn: to shout]
从戌从口。

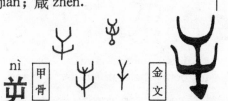 

nì 屰 [甲骨] [金文] [篆文] [参考]

— archaic form of 逆 nì: contrary; to go against; inverse
逆 nì; 朔, 蒴, 搠, 槊 shuò; 塑, 溯 sù; 嗍 suō.

* An inverted man who, perhaps, was defeated on the battlefield.   [大 dà]
象倒人形。

fá 伐 [甲骨] [金文] [古文] [篆文]

— to fell, cut down; to send a punitive expedition
筏, 阀 fá.

* An enemy being killed by a ge-halberd.
[人 rén, 戈 gē]
以戈击杀人形。

163

6.3   To the Victor Go the Spoils   俘获与暴行

fú
孚
— to inspire confidence; to trust
俘,浮,莩,桴,蜉,fú; 孵 fū;
莩,殍 piǎo.

* Seizing a child as a trophy. PLC, 俘 **fú**: prisoner of war.   [爪 zhǎo: claw, 子 zǐ: son]
以手俘获儿童形。

qǔ
取
— to take, get, obtain; to aim for
娶 qǔ: to marry (a woman);
趣 qù; 陬,鲰,诹 zōu; 聚 jù; 骤
zhòu; 最,蕞 zuì; 撮 cuō.

* A hand holding the left ear of a war prisoner. In ancient times, the left ears of war prisoners and corpses were lopped off as testimony to military exploits.
[耳 ěr, 又 yòu, 馘 guó: a prisoner of war with his left ear cut off]

手持人耳形。中国古代常采用割取敌人左耳的方法计数献功。

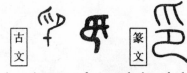

yìn
印
— to print; a seal; mark, print
昂 áng; 仰 yǎng; 抑 yì; 迎 yíng.

* A prisoner of war being held down by a hand. PLC, 抑 **yì**: to bend (head), concede; with a hand-radical. Compare the "hand" in 印 **yìn** and 抑 **yì**.
[爪 zhǎo, 卩 jié]
用手制服战俘形。

jí
及
—to reach, come up to ; in time for
汲,岌,笈,级,(极＝極)jí;
圾 jī; 吸 xī.

* A hand catching a person or enemy.
[人 rén, 又 yòu]
象手逮人形。

164

jiā 夾＝夹 甲骨 金文 古文 篆文

— to press from both sides; to clip; to mingle

＃ 浹 jiā；夹，荚，蛱，颊，郏，铗 jiá；夹 gā；悭，箧 qiè；陕 shǎn；侠，峡，狭 xiá；瘗 yì.

* Two small people (prisoners) being held under a big person's arms. PLC, 挟 xié: to hold sth. under one's arm; coerce.　[大 dà, 人 rén]

象人腋下夹有两小人形。或二人夹辅一人形。

bìng 并 甲骨 金文 篆文 篆文

— side by side ; and; to combine, merge

＃ 摒 bìng；并 bīng；饼，屏 bǐng；迸 bèng；碰 pèng: to touch, meet；胼，骈 pián；姘，拼 pīn；屏，瓶 píng.

* Two prisoners of war, their legs being tied together with sticks.　[人 rén]

并表示将两战俘的腿绑连在一起。

qiú 囚 甲骨 篆文

—to imprison; convict

＃ 泅 qiú.

* A prisoner in jail.　[人 rén]

象囚人之形。

kòu 寇 金文 古文 篆文

— bandit, invader; to invade

＃ 蔻 kòu.

* A hand holding a stick to hit a person in his room. [六 liù or 宀 mián, 元 yuán, 父 fù or 殳 shū]

象持棒进屋击人之形。

yāng 央 甲骨 金文 古文 篆文

— to entreat; centre; end

＃ 殃，秧，鸯 yāng；怏 yàng；盎 àng；英，瑛 yīng；映 yìng.

* A man being locked up in a cangue or pillory. PLC, 殃 yāng: misfortune.　[人 rén, 歹 dǎi]

戴枷的人形。

duī 𠂤

— archaic form of 師＝师 shī：
troops, army; division.

＃ 帥＝帅 shuài：commander；
師＝师：army, division, 獅
shī；篩 shāi；蟖 sī；追 duī,
zhuī.

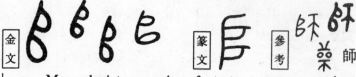

* May depict a pair of testes; one prevalent explanation is that this character is drawing of buttocks. As a symbol used in Chinese paleography, 𠂤 **duī** indicates certain military affairs such as an establishment, garrison, or force station. See below.

象睾丸之形, 在古文字中作为一种与军事有关的符号。

xuē 薛

— a surname

＃ 孽, 糱 niè.

* The testes of a prisoner of war being cut off by a 辛 **xīn**：a *xin*-sword, an ancient torture instrument. PLC, 孽 niè：evil, sin.　[𠂤 duī, 辛 xīn]

用刀割取敌方俘虏睾丸。

qiǎn 遣

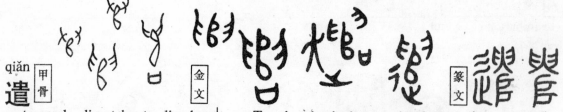

— to send, dispatch; to dispel, expel

＃ 遣, 缱 qiǎn.

* Two hands placing a pair of testes (on an altar). [又 yòu, 𠂤 duī, 辶 chuò]

双手持𠂤 (进献)。

guān 官

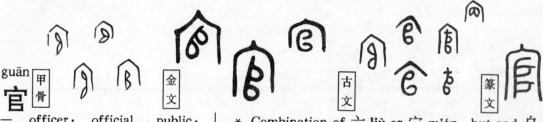

— officer; official, public; organ

＃ 倌, 棺 guān；管, 馆 guǎn；逭 huàn；菅 jiān；绾 wǎn.

* Combination of 六 liù or 宀 mián：hut and 𠂤 **duī**：a symbol for military affairs. PLC, 馆 **guǎn**：accommodation for an army (or other guests).

从宀从𠂤, 表示军旅途中止息之馆舍。

xiàn
縣=县
— county

悬 xuán；縣 dào.

* The head of an enemy hung from a tree. Here, the eye, 目 mù, represents the head. It was an ancient form of revenge to display an enemy's head on a tree, exposing it to public view. PLC, 縣=悬 xuán：to hang, suspend in midair.

[首 shǒu，系 xì：to tie，木 mù]

县即悬字初文,表示枭(xiāo)首示众。

jǐn
堇
— only

僅=仅，瑾，谨，馑 jǐn；觐 jìn；勤 qín；鄞 yín；艱=艰 jiān；漢=汉 hàn；難=难 nán，nàn；滩,摊,瘫 tān；嘆=叹 tàn.

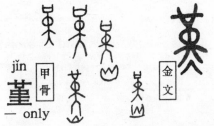

* A prisoner of war being tied up and then burnt, as an offering to bring rain. PLC.　　[大 dà，火 huǒ]

焚人牲。

màn
曼
— prolonged；graceful

漫，慢，蔓，幔，谩 màn；蔓，谩，馒，鳗 mán.

* Two hands holding an eye open. PLC.

[目 mù，又 yòu，冒 mào]

象以双手张目之形。

zāng
臧
— good, right

臧=赃 zāng；臟=脏，藏 zàng；藏 cáng.

* A ge-halberd jabbing into an enemy's eye. The left part 爿 pán is an ancient phonetic element. PLC.

[目 mù，臣 chén，戈 gē，爿 pán]

以戈伤目。臧字从戈从臣,会臧获之意,故训善。

mín
民

— the people; folk; civilian;

泯,抿 mǐn; 眠 mián.

* An eye being stabbed by a needle. The "eye ball" has been removed from the eye-socket. PLC. [目 mù]

用针刺瞎眼睛而致盲。

xīn
辛
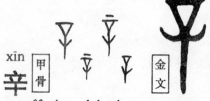

— suffering; laborious; pungent

锌 xīn; 莘 shēn; 宰 zǎi; to slaughter, butcher; 滓,梓 zǐ; 新 xīn; 亲 qīn.

* An ancient torture instrument, perhaps a kind of sword. The top part of this pictograph is used in some characters to indicate someone being tortured, see below.

古代刑具象形。

qiè
妾

— concubine

接 jiē; 霎 shà.

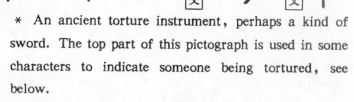

* A *xin*-sword resting on a woman's head. [辛 xīn, 女 nǚ]

刑余之女奴。

tóng
童
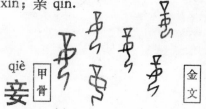

- child; virgin; a surname

隹 潼, 瞳 tóng; 憧, 艟 chōng; 鐘 = 钟 zhōng; 僮, 撞, 幢 zhuàng.

* A man's eye being gouged out with a *xin*-sword. 東 = 东 dōng in the character's ancient form was supposably a phonetic component. Later, the 目 mù: eye, and 东 dōng were merged in element 立 lì: a simplified form of 辛 xīn. PLC. [目 mù, 辛 xīn]

用辛(刑具)刺目。

xìng
幸
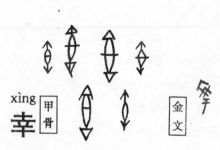  

— luck; a surname

倖 xìng; 圄 yǔ; 報 = 报 bào.

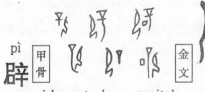

zhí

執 = 执

— to hold in the hand; to carry out, execute

縶 zhí; 挚, 贽, 鸷 zhì; 势 shì; 褻 xiè; 蛰 zhé.

* Ancient handcuffs. PLC.
古代手铐之形。

* A man being led away in handcuffs.
象戴手铐的人形。

[幸 xìng]

pì

辟

— punishment; law; capital

辟, 避, 壁, 襞, 臂, 璧 bì; 擘 bò; 臂 bèi; 劈, 擗, 霹 pī; 劈, 擗, 癖 pǐ; 僻, 譬 pì.

* A prisoner being tortured with a *xin*-sword.
[尸 shī, 口 kǒu, 辛 xīn]
用辛刀施肉刑。

xíng

刑

— punishment

型 xíng; 荆 jīng.

* Shows crisscross incisions made by a knife. 井 **jing** is also a phonetic element.   [井 jǐng, 刀 dāo]
刑字中"开"源于"井",表示刀割的伤口,也是声符。

The following characters come from an ancient practice—marriage by capture.
下列汉字可能反映了古代抢婚制的风俗。

wēi

威

— impressive strength; by force

葳, 嵗 wēi.

* A woman kneeling beneath an ax. The woman is threatened by force. PLC.
[戌 xū: a battle-ax, 女 nǚ: woman]
女在斧下之形。

nú
奴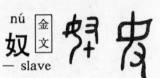
— slave
驽 nú；努，弩 nǔ；怒 nù；呶 náo；帑 tǎng.

* A woman being captured by a hand.
[女 nǔ，又 yòu]
以手抓女之形。

tuǒ
妥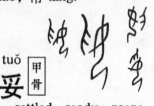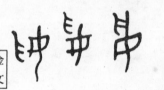
— settled, ready; prope
馁 něi；荽 suī；绥 suí.

* Shows a woman being pressed down by a hand. PLC.   [爪 zhǎo：claw，又 yòu，女 nǔ，安 ān]
以手抑女之形。

mǐn
敏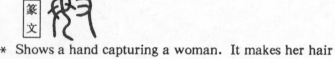
— nimble, agile
鳘 mǐn，繁 fán.

* Shows a hand capturing a woman. It makes her hair stand on end. 每 **měi** is also a phonetic. PLC.
[每 měi，父 fù]
象掠夺长发妇女之形。从攴每声，训敏疾。

qī
妻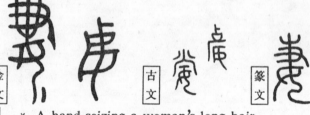
— wife
凄，萋 qī；妻 qì：(of a woman) marry.

* A hand seizing a woman's long hair.
[又 yòu，女 nǔ，夫 fū：husband]
以手抓住妇女长发之形。

lóu
婁＝娄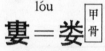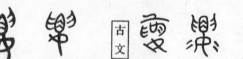
— a surname
偻，喽，楼，蝼，耧，髅 lóu；搂 lōu：to hold up；搂：to hold in one's arms, bug, embrace，嵝，篓 lǒu.

* Shows a woman being captured by hands. PLC.
[女 nǔ，又 yòu，要 yào]
双手抓女之形。

Chapter 7

FROM CULT TO CULTURE　从神化到文化

7.1　Primitive Art　原始艺术

According to archeological discoveries, early Chinese, like today's aborigines, eagerly sought communication with God. They pried out their teeth, tattooed themselves and danced with masks for God's blessing, as well as for fun. Rituals were performed for their magic efficacy in totem feasts, hunting and harvesting. Primitive art existed in their dances, music, crafts, rituals and magic. The characters in this section help to show us the shrouded marvels of Chinese Neolithic culture and art. Later, in the Chinese Bronze Age, these rituals were replaced by the complicated ceremonies of sacrifice.

通过考古发掘展现在现代人面前的中国原始艺术是丰富多彩的,然而蕴藏在汉字中的史前中国人的艺术,他们的技艺与舞蹈,他们的各式各样的仪式与巫术使人感受到的却是史前中国人的艺术冲动和同神灵交往的强烈愿望。

7.1.1—Neolithic Pottery Culture
史前陶艺

▶ The Banpo human face design and fish design.
半坡人面鱼纹展开图。
(采自《西安半坡》,
180 页。)

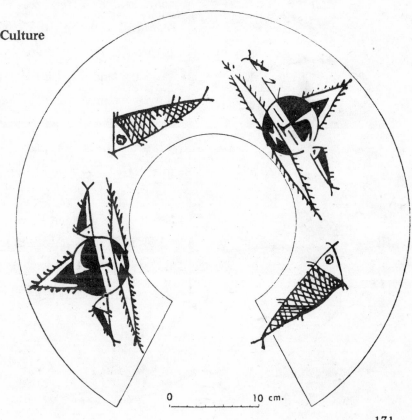

0　　　　　　10 cm.

Use of pottery is a feature of Neolithic society. The following characters reveal the Neolithic pottery culture of China, including the famous Yangshao painted pottery culture and some typically Chinese clay vessels.

wū
巫   甲骨 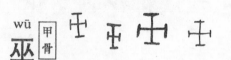   金文 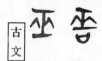   古文   篆文

— shaman; wizard

诬 wū; 靈＝灵 líng: spirit; 噬, 筮 shì.

▼ **Painted pottery ritual vessels with face motifs, Yangshao culture. Excavated at Banpo near Xi'an.**

人面鱼纹彩陶盆,西安半坡出土。

* This character derives from the character for "five", 五 **wǔ**.　〔五 wǔ〕

The painted pottery at the site of a large Neolithic village at Banpo near Xi'an was one of the main focuses of attention in 1953 and 1959 when that settlement site, dated around 5000 BC, was excavated. Some ritual potteries were found with painted patterns in various motifs. The composite designs of human faces and fish are the most intriguing among those motifs. The face designs appear on the inner walls of pottery basins which have curving rims. The designs have some subtle differences; however, the mouths are identical. The mouth's outline is in the form of a prehistoric 五 **wǔ**: five. When early Chinese designed this face and called it *wu* — a wizard, the character 巫 **wū**, meaning "wizard", had not been created, so the number five 五 **wǔ** was borrowed to indicate the wizard. The "五" placed on the mouth seems to be uttering, "我是巫 (I am a wizard)". Later, the ancient form of 五 **wǔ** was rotated 45 degrees, giving rise to the character 巫 **wū**.

巫可能源于五。半坡出土的采陶中有一种人面鱼纹图,其中人嘴的轮廓为五字的古字形,即借五为巫,指明所画为当时的巫师的面孔。

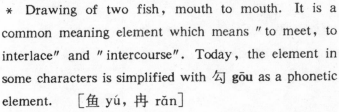

gòu 甲骨
菁

— archaic form of 構＝构 gòu：
to compose

沟，篝，轉 gōu；构，购，
媾：coition，coitus，遘 gòu；講
＝讲 jiǎng：to speak.

* Drawing of two fish, mouth to mouth. It is a common meaning element which means "to meet, to interlace" and "intercourse". Today, the element in some characters is simplified with 勾 gōu as a phonetic element. 　［鱼 yú，冉 rǎn］

The double fish design portrays another feature of the painted pottery culture. The fish appeared in face motifs containing 巫 wū. Many articles of painted pottery with double fish designs were discovered at some Neolithic sites near rivers. The location of these settlements probably accounts for the popularity of the motifs about fish. These pottery vessels with decorative patterns are more appropriate to ceremonial use than everyday use. It has been suggested that the double fish motif is a symbol for the vulva, and the fish is a prehistoric cult object for efficacy. In the Chinese symbology, the fish represents woman, because it bears a large number of eggs in its body.

象嘴对嘴的两条鱼形，在中国彩陶艺术中有一种双鱼的图案被认为是表现女阴；彩陶人面鱼纹中也有双鱼的形象。史前可能用崇拜多子的鱼的方式来祈求女子多产。一说象两个竹编器对接，见冉字。

◀ Double fish design on painted pottery vessel. It may be the emblem of a vulva. Yangshao culture.

鱼蛙纹盆。仰韶文化。

173

lì

甲骨　金文　古文　篆文

鬲

— *li*-cauldron

鬲，隔，嗝，膈，镉 gé；融 róng；獻 = 献 xiàn.

* A prehistoric earthenware pot with three hollow legs.　[豆 dòu]

In Chinese prehistoric art, it is hard to find a Stone Age idol like the "Venus" of Willendorf, a fertility image with the breasts and buttocks accentuated. However, prehistoric Chinese also wondered about the mystery of sex, which appeared to be centered in the woman's reproductive organs. There is evidence of both implicit and explicit interest in sex — 鬲 lì: a prehistoric pottery tripod with bulbous or breast-shaped hollow legs. The *li*-cauldron is a Chinese earthenware pot. This kind of vessel has been unearthed from many sites in China. Because of its large heating surface, the *li*-cauldron was a good tool for cooking. It is also an embryonic form of the famous bronze tripod. The reader can liken it to the "Venus" of Willendorf. Both of them are steatopygous, but the *li* is more exaggerated and abstract. You may also feel that the potter's veiled feelings lurk within the cauldron, whose shape may perhaps reveal traces of a once matriarchal society.

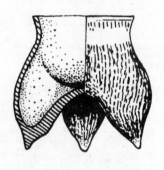

鬲是中国特有的新石器时代陶器，在鬲的基础上发展出一种以中空乳房状三足为基本特征的陶器系列。如果我们把鬲与欧洲石器时代的"维纳斯"偶象比较，会发现鬲是一种更抽象、更夸张的，具有表现力的人体艺术品。在这种陶器中或许蕴藏有史前女性崇拜的秘密。

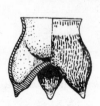

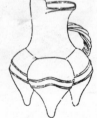

7. 1. 2—What Song the Chinese Sang
史前音乐

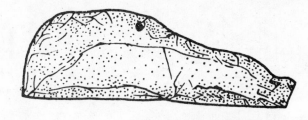

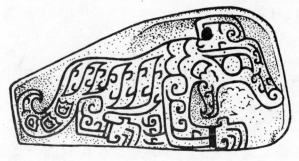

► *Above*. Chipped chime-stone. Longshan culture, the Neolithic. The stone is almost a meter high.

打制大石磬。山西襄汾陶寺遗址出土,龙山文化。

Below. Chime-stone with the tiger motif engraved on the both sides, Shang Dynasty.

虎纹石磬,商代。

W 91

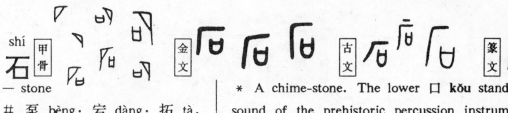

shí 石 甲骨 — stone

\# 泵 bèng; 宕 dàng; 拓 tà, tuò; 岩 yán: rock.

金文 古文 篆文

* A chime-stone. The lower 口 **kǒu** stands for the sound of the prehistoric percussion instrument. See below. It is a radical for stone or ore.   [厂 hàn]

象石磬之形,"口"表示石磬发出的声音。

qìng 磬 甲骨 — *qing*-bell, chime-stone

\# 磬 qǐng; 罄 qìng; 聲 = 声 shēng: sound; 馨 xīn.

篆文

* Shows a suspended *qing*-bell or chime-stone being struck with a mallet held by a hand. The bottom 石 **shí** is a later addition. The instrument, with varying pitches of chime-stones, is ancient and goes back to Neolithic times, but originally it appears to have consisted of only one stone.   [殳 shū: mace]

象手持槌击磬之形。

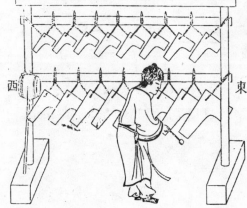

◄ 击磬。

175

yòng 用 甲骨

— use, apply; need; expenses
佣 yòng;（佣＝傭，痈＝癰，
擁＝拥 yōng）.

金文　古文　篆文

* May be a drawing of a prehistoric bell made from bamboo. PLC. See below.

可能象史前打通竹节的竹筒之形,竹筒可用来敲击发声。

yǒng 甬 金文

— a bronze bell
俑，勇，恿，涌，蛹，踊＝
踊 yǒng; 诵 sòng; 通 tōng; 桶，
捅 tǒng; 痛 tòng.

古文　篆文

* An ancient bronze bell with a ring on the handle to suspend it by.

象甬钟之形。

▶ **Rubbing of a stone from a tomb, Han Dynasty.**
汉画像石・击甬钟。

nán 南 甲骨　金文　古文　篆文

— south
喃，楠 nán; 腩 nǎn;（献＝
獻 xiàn）.

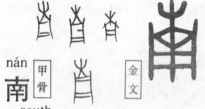

* An ancient suspended percussion instrument. PLC.
象悬挂着的一种古代打击乐器。

ké 殼 甲骨　金文　篆文

— archaic form of 殼＝壳 ké;
shell
觳 gòu; 穀＝谷，穀 gǔ; 觳
hú; 殼＝壳 ké, qiào; 慤＝悫
què.

* A hand holding a mallet to strike an ancient percussion instrument. PLC. [南 nán, 殳 shū: mace]
象手持槌击打乐器之形。

zhù

壴 甲骨

— archaic character

嘉 jiā；澍，樹＝树 shù；厨，櫥，躕 chú.

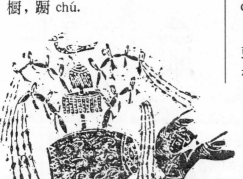

* An upright drum—*jian*-drum, an ancient ritual instrument. The drum was mounted on a long pole and decorated with a kind of plume. See below.

象建鼓之形。建鼓是一种立起来从两侧击打的鼓，鼓的下面有支架，并有木柱穿过鼓身，木柱上部带有大量装饰。

Jian-drum. Rubbing of a stone and two bricks, Han Dynasty. 汉代画像石、砖·击建鼓。

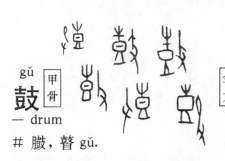

gǔ

鼓 甲骨

— drum

臌，瞽 gǔ.

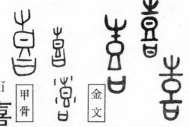

* A hand holding a drumstick to beat the drum.
象手持鼓槌击鼓之形。

xǐ

喜 甲骨 金文 古文 篆文

— happiness, joy; to like, be fond of; happy, pleased; concerning weddings

禧 xǐ；嘻，嬉，熹 xī.

* A drum and its base.
象建鼓和基座之形。

▶ Bronze drum, Shang.
商代青铜鼓。

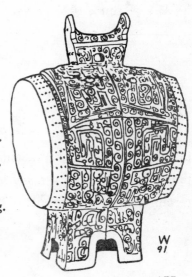

W 91

péng
彭 甲骨 金文 古文 篆文

— a surname

澎 pēng；澎，膨，蟛 péng.

* Indicates the sound of a drum. PLC.
彭表示鼓声。

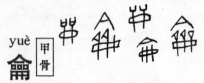

yuè
龠 甲骨 金文 篆文

— an ancient short flute.

瀹，鑰＝钥 yuè；钥 yào；籲
＝吁 yù.

* An ancient panpipe. The upper
element, a later addition, could be
the mouth playing the panpipe.
象排箫或所谓的"潘神笛"之形。

▶ Bone flute. Peiligang culture, the Neolithic. Length 22.2cm.
骨笛。裴李岗文化，新石器时代，河南舞阳贾湖遗址出土。该骨笛是
同遗址出土十六支骨笛中最完整无裂纹的一支，并有测音研究报告。

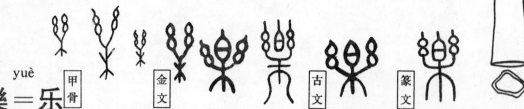

yuè
樂＝乐 甲骨 金文 古文 篆文

— music

樂＝乐 lè；cheerful；栎，砾
lì；烁，铄 shuò；藥＝药 yào.

* Two strings fastened to a plank, an attempt to
represent a stringed instrument. The upper middle 白
bái, pictograph of a thumb, was added later as a
meaning element. [丝 sī：silk，木 mù：wood，白 bái]
象古代的弦乐器。

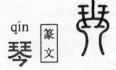

qín
琴 篆文

— a seven-stringed plucked
instrument in some ways similar
to the zither; a general name for
certain musical instruments

* An ancient zither. The lower part 今 **jīn** is a
phonetic element added later.
[琵琶 pípā：a plucked string instrument with a fretted
fingerboard；瑟 sè：a long stringed instrument,
originally with 5 or 10 strings, later 25 strings]
象古琴形。今为声符。

7. 1. 3—The Body in Art　史前人体艺术

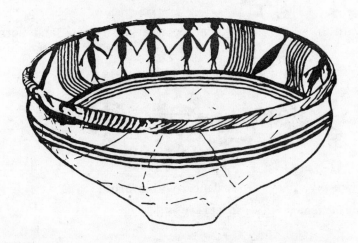

A 5000-year-old pottery bowl from Qinghai Province. It is painted with a ring of 15 dancers, adorned in headdresses and sashes and stepping in unison (*after Zhu, D. p.* 534).

舞蹈彩盆。青海大通出土。

wén

文　甲骨

— writing, character, script; language; literary, composition; culture; civilian; gentle

\# 雯, 纹, 蚊 wén; 紊 wěn; (坟 = 墳 fén); 吝 lìn; 虔 qián.

金文　　　古文　　篆文

* A person with a tattoo on his chest. PLC，纹 wén: weins, grain.　　[文身 wénshēn: tattoo]

象有文身图案的人形。

wú

無 = 无　甲骨

— nothing; not have; not

\# 芜 wú; 妩, 怃, 庑 wǔ; 抚 fú.

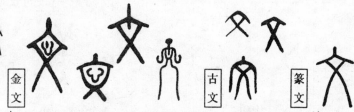

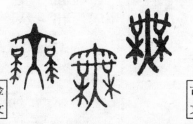

金文　　古文　　篆文

* A dancer with props — perhaps holding two ox tails. PLC，舞 wǔ: to dance; the lower part of 舞 wǔ derives from the dancer's feet.　　[大 dà]

象手持物而舞的人形。

179

jì  金文 篆文

冀

— to hope, look forward to

\# 骥 jì.

* A dancer wearing a mask and horn ornaments. PLC.　[异 yì]

戴有面具和角饰跳舞的人形。

yì 甲骨 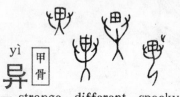 金文 古文 篆文

异

— strange, different, spooky

\# 翼 yì；戴 dài；冀＝粪 fèn.

* A dancer with a mask. PLC.　[鬼 guǐ]

戴面具跳舞的人形。

měi 甲骨 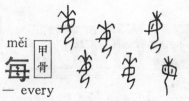 金文 古文 篆文

每

— every

\# 海 hǎi；悔 huǐ；晦，海 huì；莓，梅，酶，霉 méi；侮 wǔ；毓 yù.

* A woman wearing a feather headdress. PLC.

[母 mǔ, 美 měi]

戴羽毛头饰的女子。

měi 甲骨 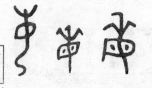 金文 古文 篆文

美

— beauty; beautiful

\# 镁 měi.

* A man with a feather headdress, a chief of a tribe. PLC.　[每 měi, 大 dà]

戴羽饰的男子形。

hēi 金文  古文 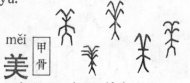 篆文 参考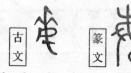

黑

— black

\# 嘿 hēi；墨，默 mò.

* Picture of a dancer wearing a mask and some ornaments, or perhaps covered with warpaint or branding on his face and body. Later, the dancer's body was separated from the head, and the lower parts transformed into a fire-radical. Burns are often black.

[舞 wǔ, 大 dà, 火 huǒ]

象头戴面具跳舞的人形。

lín 粦

金文

— ancient form of 磷 lín: will-o'-the-wisp; phosphorescent light; phosphorum

\# 憐＝怜 lián；鄰＝邻，遴，嶙，瞵，辚，麟，鳞 lín；膦 lìn.

篆文

* A pictograph of a dancer holding props in his hands. Later, this character represented a ghost dancing between grave mounds with a jack-o'-lantern.

[舞 wǔ，黑 hēi，火 huǒ]

象舞蹈的人形。此字又用于指"鬼火"。

guǐ 鬼

甲骨 金文 古文 篆文

— ghost, spook

\# 瑰 guī；槐 huái；魂 hún；塊＝块 kuài；魁 kuí；傀 kuǐ；愧 kuì；魄 pò；嵬 wéi；隗 wěi，kuí；醜＝丑 chǒu.

* A figure with a mask and a tail ornament. See above.

戴面具和尾饰的人形。

wèi 畏

甲骨 金文 古文 篆文

— fear; awe

\# 喂 wèi；偎，隈 wēi；猥 wěi.

* A "ghost" dancing with a stick. PLC.

[鬼 guǐ，长 cháng]

象"鬼"持棒而舞。

The following characters may be related to the harvest dances. Early Chinese men, women, and children, danced with rice headdresses. In these characters, 禾 hé: rice is a common element.

nián 年

甲骨 金文 古文 篆文

— year; the times; condition of harvest

* A man wearing a rice headdress performing a dance to celebrate the harvest. [人 rén，千 qiān]

象人头顶禾谷，表示丰收。

jì
季
— season
悸 jì.

* Drawing of a child wearing a rice headdress. PLC.
象用禾为头饰的儿童。

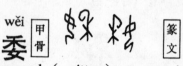

wěi
委
— end (written); to appoint, send
诿，萎，巍，逶 wēi；诿，痿，萎 wěi；魏 wèi；矮 ǎi；倭 wō.

* A combination of 禾 **hé**: rice, and 女 **nǔ**: woman. PLC.　[禾 hé，女 nǔ]
禾与女的组合。

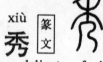

xiù
秀
— delicate, frail and beautiful; to flower
绣，锈 xiù；透 tòu；莠 yǒu；诱 yòu.

* A combination of rice and a pictograph of the breasts. Both of them were considered to have magic efficacy.　[禾 hé，乃 nǎi]
禾与乃的组合。"乃"是乳房的象形。

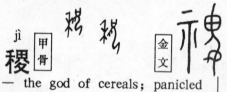

jì
稷
— the god of cereals; panicled millet
谡 sù.

* A man praying before rice.　[兄 xiōng，鬼 guǐ]
象人在禾前祈祷之形。

182

7.2 Divination and Sacrificial Offerings 占卜与祭祀

7.2.1—Divination 占卜

Superstition was extensive in ancient China, so that the early Chinese held frequent divining ceremonies. They consulted oracles about everything from the timing of sacrifices and military compaigns to pleas for rain and cures for disease.

The main materials used in divination were the cow's shoulder blade and turtle's shell. At the moment of divination, the king's diviner first recorded the charge or marginal notation which detailed the question and purpose of a given divination. It was then inscribed onto the surface of the bone and shell. After that, a series of hollow pits were bored or chiselled into the back or inner surface of the bone or shell. Heat was then applied to the hollow pits. Scorching of the bone or shell caused ⼘-shaped cracks to fan out on the surface. The hollow pits decreased the thickness of the bone or shell, making it easier to crack. Once the crack formed, they were presumably " read" by the diviner or the king himself. Sometimes, especially if the result was efficacious, it was also inscribed onto the bone or shell near the original charge.

The bones and shells are called oracle bones, and a great number of the antiques of Shang Dynasty were unearthed in Henan Province about 100 years ago. In 1977 and 1979, many oracle bones of West Zhou Dynasty came to light at *Zhouyuan*, in Shaanxi Province. The writings carved on the bones or shells are known as oracle bone inscriptions.

▶ A turtle plastron and a bovid scapula used in divination (*after Li, Xueqin* (1) *p*. 25).
殷墟卜用龟腹甲和牛胛骨。

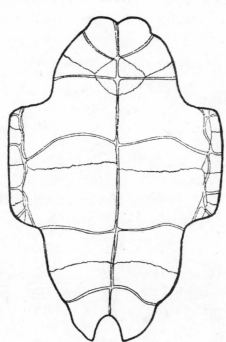
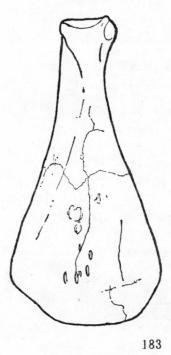

xū 需 甲骨  金文  篆文 需
— to need, want
儒，孺，蠕，薷，顬，嚅，濡 rú.

* A priest or diviner taking a shower before performing divination or other ritual. PLC, 濡 **rú**: to immerse.

[亦 yǐ, 雨 yǔ, 而 ér and 儒 rú: learned man]

象人沐浴之形。古人占卜或祭祀之前要进行沐浴，以示诚敬。

bǔ 卜 甲骨 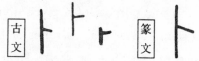 金文 古文 篆文 卜
— to divine; predict, foretell; divination; a surname
(补＝補 bǔ)；讣，赴 fù；咎 jiù；钋 pō；朴 pò；外 wài；(扑＝撲 pū；仆＝僕 pú；朴＝樸 pǔ).

* Portrays the 卜-shaped crack formed on the oracle bone or shell.

甲骨上烧灼而成的卜兆。

guǎ 冎 甲骨 古文 篆文
— to scrape meat off bone (archaic)
剐 guǎ；骨 gū；gǔ；埚，锅，涡 guō；過＝过 guò；滑，猾 huá；祸 guò；娲 wā；挝，涡，莴，窝，蜗 wō.

* Drawing of the cow's shoulder blade used for divination. Note the small 卜 **bǔ** on the bone. PLC, 骨 **gǔ**; bone; with a human body radical. 骨 **gǔ** is also a radical.   [卜 **bǔ**; 肉 **ròu**]

象占卜用牛胛骨之形。在骨上有卜纹。

dǎi 歹 甲骨 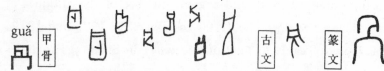 篆文 参考  死
— bad, wicked; bad deed
死 sǐ: to die; 歺 sù.

* Drawing of a rotten bone. It may derive from 骨 **guǎ**, see above. 歹 **dǎi** is a radical.

象残骨之形。

zhēn 貞＝贞 甲骨 金文 古文 篆文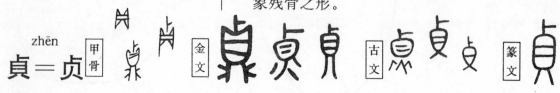

— divination; loyal, faithful;
(of woman) chastity or virginity
侦，祯，桢 zhēn；帧 zhèng.

* A kind of bronze tripod used for heating the bronze rod and to scorch the bone or shell during divination. The upper part 卜 **bǔ** indicates the use of the bronze tripod. 贝 **bèi** is the simplified form of 鼎 **dǐng**：tripod.

[朕 zhèn]

从鼎从卜。鼎在占卜中用于烧灼加热。

zhēn
真
— true, real; clearly
缜 zhěn；镇 zhèn；嗔 chēn；
滇，颠，巅，癫 diān.

* This common character derives from 贞 zhēn；真人 **zhēnrén** (literally "true man") meant wizard.

真源于贞。

shòu
受 甲骨
— to receive, accept
授，绶 shòu.

* Depicts the taking or delivering of a divination plate by hands. Later, the plate was simplified. When a bone or tortoise shell was ready to be used or accepted by the oracle, it was placed on a large plate. No person was then allowed to touch the bone or shell.

[授 shòu：award, teach，爪 zhǎo，又 yòu]

受表示用手传递放有占卜用甲骨的大盘。一说用手传递舟，形声兼会意字。

zhèn
朕 甲骨
— sign, omen; I, the sovereign
胜＝胜 shèng；腾＝誊，滕，藤，腾 téng；媵 yìng；送 sòng：to give.

* Shows the diviner holding a heated bronze rod to scorch the bone or shell in order to form the crack. The left-hand part 月 **yuè** derives from the drawing of the divination plate.　[受 shòu]

朕字右边的关表示占卜者双手持加热的青铜棒，左边的月源于占卜时放置甲骨的大盘。朕字表示烧灼甲骨以形成卜兆。

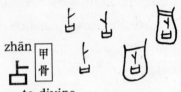

zhān — to divine

沾，毡，粘 zhān；站，（战＝戰）zhàn；觇 chān；掂 diān；點＝点，踮 diǎn；店，惦，阽，坫，玷 diàn；乩 jī；拈 niān；黏＝粘，鲇＝ nián；苫 shān；帖，萜，贴 tiē；帖 tiě，tiè；砧 zhēn；（钻＝鑽 zuān，zuàn）．

* Drawing of the 卜-shaped crack on a scapula or shoulder blade of ox combined with a small 口 kǒu: mouth, means to ask the oracle.   [卜 bǔ]

在卜骨上形成卜兆，并询问结果。

7. 2. 2—Sacrificial Offerings   祭祀

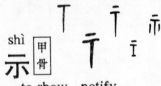

shì 示 — to show, notify

（标＝標 biāo；际＝際 jì）．

* A T-shaped sacrificial altar, or an abstract symbol of the narrow, ghostly Hell and the broad, bright Heaven (see the scenes on the silk-painting). The three strokes surrounding the "T" were later additions, used to balance or beautify the T-shaped altar.

象 T 形祭台，或被解释为神主。古文字示主一字。

▶ Lady Dai's funeral banner with tassels is an illustration of the character 示 shì. The T-shaped red silk banner painting came to light from the Han Tomb No. 1 at *Mawangdui*, Changsha, Hunan Province in 1972. This banner depicts Lady Dai's ascent to heaven. The bottom section portrays the ghosts in hell and the offerings made to them. The next section shows Lady Dai and her maids, while just above her are two guardians waiting at the gate of heaven. The heavenly paradise at the top consists of the moon, the sun, two dragons and the primordial ancestor Fuxi with a long serpent tail. Lady Dai was a minor official's wife in the Han dynasty. (*From Fagan*, p. 260, *drawing by David Buck*, *copied from Changsha Mawangdui Yihao Hanmu* 1973. *Length* 205cm, *width* 92—47.7cm.)

马王堆一号汉墓出土的轪夫人升天彩绘帛画，为当时葬仪中所用的旌幡。

qiě 且 甲骨  金文  篆文

— for the time being; let alone; both. . . and. . .

锄 chú; 粗 cū; 姐 jiě; 沮, 咀, 龃 jǔ; 蛆 qū; 宜 yí; 谊 yì; 助 zhù; 租 zū; 阻, 袓, 俎, 诅 zǔ.

* A phallic-shaped altar to ancestors. PLC, 祖 zǔ: ancestor (acc. Bernhard Karlgen).　[士 shì, 示 shì]

象牡器形状的祭台。

jì 祭 甲骨 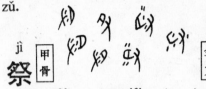 金文  古文 篆文

— to offer a sacrifice to; to wield

* Portrays a hand placing a piece of pork on the altar. [肉 ròu, 又 yòu, 示 shì]

用手将肉放在祭台上。

zōng 宗 甲骨 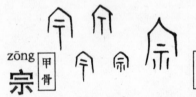 金文  古文 篆文

— ancestral temple, ancestor, clan

棕，腙，综，鬃，踪 zōng; 粽 zòng; 崇 chóng; 淙，琮 cóng.

* Shows an altar inside the ancestral temple. [六 liù or 宀 mián, 示 shì]

宗庙中的祭台。

xiōng 兄 甲骨 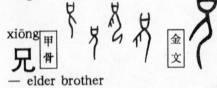 金文  古文 篆文

— elder brother

贶，况 kuàng; 祝 zhù.

* A person facing the sky and praying. The direction of mouth indicates the upward face. PLC. 祝 zhù: wish, hope.　[示 shì, 兑 duì, 欠 qiàn]

象人仰面张口祈祷形。

mǐn 皿 甲骨  金文 古文 篆文 参考 盥

— vessel, utensil

盥 guàn: to wash hands.

* A plate or vessel with a tall pedestal and attached handles. 皿 mǐn is a lower radical for vessels.

象有耳高足的器皿形。

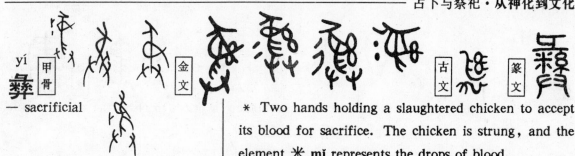

yí

彝

— sacrificial

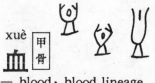

甲骨 金文 古文 篆文

* Two hands holding a slaughtered chicken to accept its blood for sacrifice. The chicken is strung, and the element 米 **mǐ** represents the drops of blood.

[彖 tuàn，糸 mì，又 yòu or 共 gòng]

以鸡为牺,杀鸡取血用于祭祀。

xuè

血

— blood；blood lineage

\# 血 xiě；恤，洫 xù.

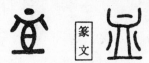

甲骨 古文 篆文

* Drawing shows a dot on a ritual vessel. The dot represents the blood used for sacrificial rites. [皿 mǐn]

象盛血的祭盘。

mèng

孟

— eldest（brother）；the first monty（of a season）；a surname

\# 猛，锰，蜢，艋 měng.

金文 古文 篆文

* A combination of 八 **bā**：to cut，子 **zǐ**：son and 皿 **mǐn**：a ritual vessel. Early Chinese once offered their first baby to the gods. The practice of infanticide, a callous and atrocious custom, appeared in ancient China. [八 bā，子 zǐ，皿 mǐn]

孟(从八)从子从皿。

níng

寧＝宁

— tranquil；would rather

\# 柠，拧，咛，狞 níng；拧 nǐng；宁，泞 nìng.

甲骨 金文 篆文

* A ritual vessel containing a heart on a T-shaped sacrificial altar, and being kept in a temple. The heart element appeared later；it may be a radical.

[宗 zōng，皿 mǐn，心 xīn]

象贮藏器物于室内形。

189

盡＝尽 jìn 甲骨

— to the highest degree or the utmost limit; all; to come to an end; to use up completely

烬，荩，赆 jìn; 盡＝尽 jìn.

* A hand holding a brush to clean the ritual vessel.
［聿 yù, 皿 mǐn］

手持刷子洗刷器皿之形。

義＝义 yì 甲骨

— righteousness; human relationship; adopted

议 yì; 仪 yí: ceremony; 蚁 yǐ.

* A ram being slaughtered by a saw-ax for sacrifice.
［我 wǒ, 羊 yáng, 犧＝牺 xī: sacrifice］

从羊从我，表示杀羊祭祀。

7. 3   The Cradle of Civilization   文明的摇篮

7. 3. 1—Quipu—keeping Records by Weaving Knots   结绳记事

系 xì 甲骨

— to be; system, series; relate to

繫＝系 jì: tie.

* Drawing of a hand holding a prehistoric *quipu*, a record kept by weaving patterned knots. It is a remnant of an ancient custom.   ［又 yòu or 爪 zhǎo, 糸 mì］

象史前记事的结绳。

孫＝孙 sūn 甲骨

— grandson; a surname

狲 sūn; 逊 xùn.

* A combination of 子 zǐ: son and 系 xì: quipu. The upper knot may stand for the child, while the lower knot represents the child's child.

指示子孙相承关系的结绳。

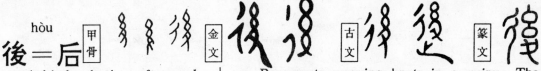

hòu

後 = 后

甲骨

金文

古文

篆文

— behind，back；afterward，later

* Represents weaving knots in a quipu. The foot symbol points in toward the weaving, and 彳 chì on the left indicates the action of weaving.

［止 zhǐ，彳 chì，后 hòu］

用结绳记事的方法指示事件发生的先后关系。

shì

世

金文

古文

篆文

— lifetime；generation；age，era；world

贯 shì；屉 tì；泄，绁 xiè.

* A quipu recording pedigree or genealogy. ［止 zhǐ］

古文字世从止声。上加三点（三划）作指示符号。又象表示家族世系的结绳形。

dōng

冬

甲骨

金文

古文

篆文

— winter

氡，咚 dōng；疼 téng；终，螽 zhōng.

* Shows the ends of a quipu. The two dots are a later addition to indicate winter. PLC，终 zhōng：end，finish；with a silk radical. ［冫 bīng］

象结绳终结形。

duō

多

甲骨

金文

古文

篆文

— many，much，more

哆 duō；眵 chī；侈 chǐ；移 yí.

* Two quipus. ［冬 dōng］

两个结绳形。

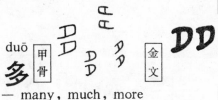

7.3.2—Numbers and Symbols　数字和符号

The earliest uses of glyphs were not to convey ideas, experience or otherwise, but to keep records of hunting, harvest, fabricated goods and booty. The arithmetical reckoning was an even greater feat than the capture.

文字的出现首先从简单的数字符号开始。汉字中还保留着中国人的祖先积画成数的原始计数方法。但是，用积画成数的方法不便于表示大的数目，因此大于四的数字就使用假借的方法来表示了。

yī
甲骨

金文

古文

篆文

一 one, a

* One stroke. This glyph is one of the most common characters in the Chinese language. The horizontal stroke is a symbol of carrying numbers，used in the units of numbers such as 十 **shí**：ten，百 **bǎi**：hundred，千 **qiān**：thousand and 萬＝万 **wàn**：ten thousand.

一画为一，一表示算筹形。在十百千万诸字中，"一"可以表示进位。

èr
甲骨

金文

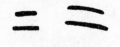

古文

篆文

二 two

＃ 仁 rén；贰 èr；腻 nì；佞 nìng；竺 zhú.

* Two strokes.
积画成二。

sān
甲骨

金文

古文

篆文

三 three

＃ 叁 sān.

* Three horizontal strokes.
积画成三。

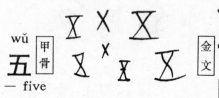

wǔ
甲骨

金文

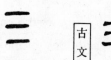

古文

篆文

五 five

＃ 伍，捂，悟 wǔ；吾，浯，梧，齬 wú；悟，晤，焐，寤，瘟 wù；衙 yá；语 yǔ.

* Creating numerals by adding strokes is a good method for 一 二 三 or one two three. But it fails when representing numbers larger than four or five. Early Chinese used a cross to indicate the number five；it has been seen on Chinese Neolithic pottery inscriptions. Note that five is the middle point between one and nine.

[四 sì：four，六 liù：six，七 qī：seven，八 bā：eight]

借叉号表示五。在中国史前陶器刻划符号中已经出现了这种叉号。

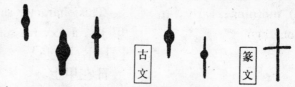

shí 甲骨 金文 古文 篆文

一 ten; topmost

\# 什 shén, shí; 廿 niàn: twenty; 卅 sà: thirty.

* At first 十 **shí** consisted of only one vertical stroke. Later, a horizontal stroke was added to carry the number. [一 yī, 七 qī]

古时一竖画代表十,后加"一"可理解为进位。

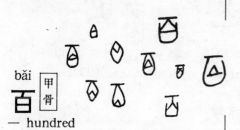

bǎi 甲骨

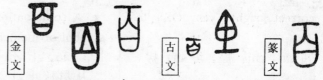

金文 古文 篆文

一 hundred

\# 佰 bǎi; 陌 mò.

* The pictograph 白 **bái** was borrowed for the unit of hundred, and "一" means to carry the number. [一 yī, 白 bái]

借白为百。百从白字分化而来。

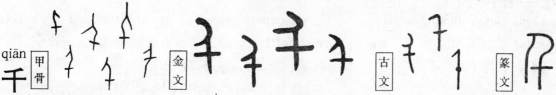

qiān 甲骨 金文 古文 篆文

一 thousand

\# 仟,阡,芊,扦,(迁=遷, 千=韆),钎 qiān;(忏=懺 chàn; 歼 jiān; 跹,纤 xiān).

* The pictograph of a man, 人 **rén**, was borrowed for the unit of thousand, and "一" means to carry the number. [人 rén, 一 yī]

借人为千,"人腿"上一画表示进位。

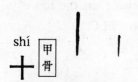

jiǎ 甲骨

金文 古文 篆文

一 a suit of armor; nail, shell; the first of the Heavenly stems

\# 岬,胛,钾 jiǎ; 呷 xiā; 匣, 狎,柙 xiá; 押,鸭 yā; 闸 zhá.

* A pole or column with a cross on its upper part as a tool for measuring the sun. PLC. [日 rì]

象上端交横木的木柱(华表),用以测日计时(日在甲中)。

zǎo 篆文

早

-- (early) morning; early, in advance; long ago

草 cǎo.

* This character shows the sun rising on the top of a 甲 jiǎ, a tool for solar observation. PLC.

[日 rì, 甲 jiǎ]

日在甲上。

shì
是

— correct, right; yes, OK; to be

匙 shi, chí; 提, 堤 dī; 提, 醍 tí.

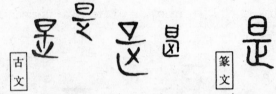

* A combination of 早 zǎo and 止 zhǐ: footprint—a symbol of moment and a phonetic too. PLC.

[早 zǎo, 止 zhǐ]

从早从止,止亦声。

shí
時 = 时

— time, days; hour; current, present

鰣 shí; 蒔 shì.

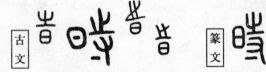

* A combination of 日 rì: the sun and 之 zhǐ: a symbol of footprint. 寺 sì is a phonetic element.

[日 rì, 之 zhī, 寺 sì, 寸 cùn]

时从日之声(后寺声),表示太阳的运动。

xī
昔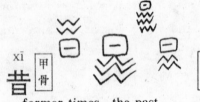

— former times, the past

腊, 惜 xī; 醋 cù; 措, 错 cuò; 籍, 藉 jí; 藉 jiè; 腊, 蜡 là; 鹊 què; 蜡 zhà.

* Derived from a prehistoric system for recording time. Perhaps early Chinese carved zigzag lines to count days. The "sun", 日 rì: day, is a meaning element.   [日 rì]

史前人类多用刻画短线来计日。昔可能源于史前的"日历"。旧以为从水从日,指过去大禹治水的往昔年代。

zhōng
中

— center, middle; China; in, among

\# 忠，盅，衷，（钟＝鐘）zhōng；（肿＝腫，种＝種 zhǒng）；中，仲，（种）zhòng；衝＝冲，忡 chōng；种 chóng；（冲 chòng）.

* Drawing of a pole with some decorative streamers. The pole was placed in the center of a circle or dial so that a shadow cast by the sun on a calibrated dial could measure solar time—much like the gnomon or style of a sundial.

　中字源于古代日晷测时树立起的杆子,即圭表测影的表。

guī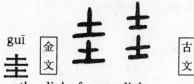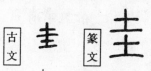

— the dial of a sundial

\# 硅，闺，鲑 guī；桂 guì；卦，挂，褂 guà；恚 huì；佳 jiā；街 jiē；奎 kuí；畦 qí；窪＝洼，哇，蛙 wā；娃 wá；哇 wa；鞋 xié.

* Shows one part or section of the graduated lines on a sundial.

　象圭上的一段刻度之形。

shàng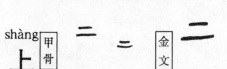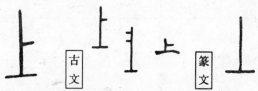

— upper, up; higher; to go up

\# 忐 tǎn；（让＝讓 ràng）.

* A dot above a horizontal stroke.

　横上一点。

xià

— down, under, below; lower; to descend

\# 吓 xià；忑 tè；卡 kǎ；（虾＝蝦 xiā）.

* A dot below a horizontal stroke.

　横下一点。

qū

— bent, crooked; unjustifiable; curve

\# 蛐，麯＝曲 qū；曲 qǔ.

* Shows a crooked or concave thing. PLC.

　象物曲折之形。

7. 3. 3—Education 教育

yáo
爻 甲骨 金文  篆文

— in *The Book of Changes* or《易经》yìjīng, the basic continuous line——（阳爻 yángyáo; male *yao*）and broken line——（阴爻 yīnyáo; female *yao*）used in divination trigrams

* The two crosses which appear also in 教 **jiāo** and 学 **xué** represent bamboo counting-rods（筹 **chóu**）. The notations by rods were of two types, and they were used consecutively. ［教 jiāo, 学 xué］

两组相交的算筹形。

Counting-rods（筹）place value

	0	1	2	3	4	5	6	7	8	9
vertical	(gap)	I	II	III	IIII	IIIII	T	TT	TTT	TTTT
horizontal	(gap)	—	=	≡	≣	≣	⊥	⊥	⊥	⊥

suàn
算 篆文

— to count; to plan, calculate; accounting; number
篡 cuàn; 纂 zuǎn; 蒜 suàn.

* Both hands calculating with some bamboo counting-rods, and the whole is topped by a bamboo-radical. In some written forms, the counting-rods resemble an abacus; however, the Chinese invented the abacus in the 14th century, not in the Han Dynasty.
［竹 zhú, 又 yòu or 共 gòng］
双手持筹计算之形。

jiāo
教 甲骨 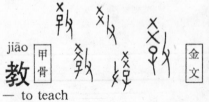 金文 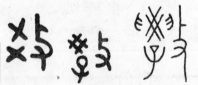 古文 篆文

— to teach
教 jiào: education, religion.

* A hand holding a pointer and teaching a child a lesson, which is designated by the two crosses 爻 **yáo**.
［爻 yáo, 子 zǐ: son, 父 fù: father］
手持教鞭教子之形。手持教鞭为"父",所指教的内容为"爻"。

xué
學＝学
— to learn
甲骨 金 篆

* A child arranging the counting-rods in a house, see above. ［教 jiāo, 爪 zhǎo, 六 liù］

象子双手持筹仿效之形。

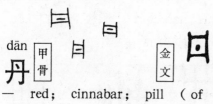
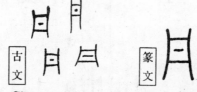

shān
甲骨 金文 篆文
— (archaic character)
杉，钐，衫 shān.

* A radical implying pattern and adornment, for instance in 彩 **cǎi**：color, pigment；影 **yǐng**：shadow；形 **xíng**：form；etc.

彡表示笔画或装饰的纹样。

dān
丹
甲骨 金文 古文 篆文
— red; cinnabar; pill (of immortality sought by alchemists), elixir vitae
坍 tān；彤 tóng.

* Shows a piece of cinnabar (the dot) placed in a tray or palette to be used as red pigment.

调色盘中放有朱砂用作红色颜料。

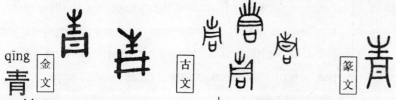

qīng
青
金文 古文 篆文
— blue or green; green grass; young (people)
清，蜻，鲭 qīng；情，晴，氰 qíng；请 qǐng；菁，腈，睛，精 jīng；静，靖 jìng；倩 qiàn.

* Represents the color of grass; the top 生 **shēng** is a pictophonetic element, the lower 丹 **dān** is a meaning element. ［生 shēng, 丹 dān：palette, 井 jǐng］

青字从生从井或丹，表示青草的颜色。

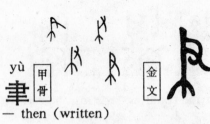

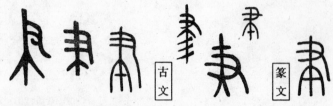

yù

聿 甲骨 金文 古文 篆文

— then (written)

\# 筆 = 笔 bǐ：pen；書 = 书
shū：to write, a book；畫 = 画
huà：to paint, a painting；律 lǜ；
建，健，犍，腱，键 jiàn；犍
jiān.

* A hand holding a Chinese writing brush. PLC.
[隶 lì]

象手持毛笔形。

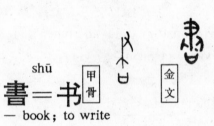

shū

書 = 书 甲骨 金文 古文 篆文 参考 畫

— book；to write

* A combination of 聿 yù：holding a writing brush
and 口 kǒu：mouth. A phonetic element 者 zhě had
been introduced in this character.   [聿 yù，口 kǒu]

从聿从口，表示记录语言。

cè

册 甲骨 金文 篆文

— book, booklet；copy

\# 删：to delete, cut out, 姗，
珊，栅，跚 shān；栅 zhà：
railings, bar.

* An ancient Chinese bamboo-slip book. Before paper
had been invented, Chinese people wrote characters on
bamboo slips and then tied them together at their ends,
forming a scroll. Therefore, Chinese developed the
habit of writing and reading vertically because of the
position of the bamboo, sometimes wood, slips.

编简成册。

diǎn

典 甲骨 金文 古文 篆文

— established or traditional system, institution or law; classic; dictionary; literary allusion or reference; a surname; to mortgage, pawn
碘 diǎn；腆 tiǎn.

* Both hands holding a 册 cè：bamboo-slip book.
[册 cè]
双手捧册之形。

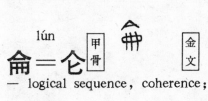

lún

侖＝仑

— logical sequence, coherence; to ponder
伦，沦，抡，囵，论，纶，轮 lún；论 lùn：to discuss, view；抡 lūn.

* 仑 lún shows 册 cè：a bamboo-slip book, placed in a room. [六 liù，册 cè]
屋下有书。

Cang Jie, the legendary inventor of Chinese writing. He got his ideas from observing the human body, plants, animals and birds as well as other natural phenomena; thus, it was said he had four eyes (*after Mao, Peiqi*).
仓颉，相传为文字始创者。

199

Design on a bronze wine jar, Warring States Period.

战国铜器图案。

后　记

　　作者近年来通过给美国来华学习汉语的学生业余讲授汉字起源,逐步整理出一些有关古文字方面的材料,并汇集成此书。

　　文字源于图画。中国文字是在图形文字的基础上衍生发展而来的。源于图形文字的汉字数量有限,但作用很大,它们不仅是占汉字总数近百分之九十的形声字的"形"的基础,也是其"声"的基础。本书主要解释这些源于图形文字的汉字,同时列出它们的形声衍生字,通过讲解汉字的起源,从图形入手,帮助以拼音文字为母语的人更快更有兴趣地学习汉字汉语。同时,本书也可作为汉字字源字典使用。在编排上,本书是以内容安排汉字,其中前两章人类与自然是全书的基础。这种编排的方法有利于学习汉字,然而对字源的解释多数情况下只能选取一种较为合理的说法。

　　书中所选的汉字不仅能够反映出中国人的祖先对人类自身和大自然的认识,也在一定程度上反映了他们在生产、生活和社会组织等方面的实践活动。同时,从这些汉字中我们可以看到先民对事物的观察是系统而精细的,这应当成为自然科学发展的良好开端。然而,中国的自然科学进入封建社会以来却逐渐背离了实践的方向。中国宋朝的朱熹曾说:"存心于一草木一器用之间,此是何学问?!为此而望有所得,是炊沙而欲其成饭也!"(《晦庵先生文集》卷三九,"答陈齐仲")……

　　在完成本书期间,一些来华学习汉语的朋友帮助编辑校订了本书的英文部分。其中 Tamar P. Shay (谢晶), Rose Jennifer, Bridie Chi (齐若颖), Dawn Anderson (安晓)和 Shannon Sweeney (沈秋兰)等人给予作者很大帮助。沈秋兰小姐和关宗湘先生校订了全书的英文部分。华语教学出版社周奎杰社长为本书的出版尽了极大的努力,中国科学院考古研究所张亚初研究员审阅了本书, 另外,考古所的刘兴光同志和中华书局的李岩同志以及傅克勤同志、程琨同志也给予作者很大帮助,在此作者对他们表示衷心的谢意。

　　本书收录繁体字以语文出版社出版的《语言文字规范手册》(增订本)为准,不收异体字。书中古文字部分是由作者用硬笔书写的。本书中文部分解释较短,国内读者应注意英文中的"PLC",表示假借字。其后如果接有汉字,则一般认为字条汉字为该字的本字。例如:求字条中求为假借字,是裘的本字。

　　利用古文字材料为对外汉语教学服务是一种新的尝试,要完善本书还有大量的工作要做。作者是在时间和材料都有限的条件下完成这一工作的,本书只能做为近三年来作者在这方面工作的一个总结,作者期待着读者的批评指教。

　　最后,让我引用何炳棣在其著作《东方的摇篮》一书最后一段文字来作为本书的结束语。

　　中国的文明是与两河流域文明一样有原始性的,而在原始性上可以宣称有同等的优先性。它不能再当做旧大陆几个"边缘性的"文明之一而加以对待了。就像两河流域很合适地被称为西方的摇篮一样,华北的黄土地区也当称为东方的摇篮。实际上,在这两个原始文明中,不妨把中国文明认为更值得注意。这是由于它独一无二的长命,它日后内容的丰富,以及它在人类三分之一之众所居住的东亚的优势的影响力。The Chinese civilization was just as pristine as the Mesopotamian and in terms of originality could claim equal primacy. It can no longer be treated as one of the several "peripheral" civilizations of the Old World. As Mesopotamia is rightly known as the cradle of the West, so the loess area of North China deserves to be called the cradle of the East. The Chinese may well be judged the more remarkable of the two pristine civilizations because of its unique longevity, the richness of its later contents, and its dominant influence over all of East Asia, whose inhabitants now account for more than one-third of humanity. (*From Ho Ping-ti, p.* 368. 中文译文选自张光直 *Chang Kwang-chih* (4), *p.* 1.)

王宏源　H. Y. WANG

May 29, 1992

Bibliography

Ancient China's Technology and Science. Beijing：Foreign Language Press，1983.

Ann，T. K. 安子介．　*Cracking the Chinese Puzzles.* Stockflows Co.，Ltd. Hongkong，1982.

Atsuji，T. 阿辻哲次：　《图说汉字的历史》，　东京：大修馆书店，1989.

Chang，Kwang-chih（1）张光直．*The Archaeology of Ancient China.* New Haven：Yale University Press.

　—（2）：《中国青铜时代》，北京：三联书店，1982。

　—（3）：《中国青铜时代（二集）》，北京：三联书店，1990。

　—（4）：《考古学专题六讲》，北京：文物出版社，1986。

Chen，Guoqiang *et al.*，*eds.* 陈国强主编：《简明文化人类学词典》　(*A Concise Dictionary of Cultural Anthropology*)，杭州：浙江人民出版社，1990。

Chen Quanfang 陈全方：《周原与周文化》(*Zhouyuan and the Zhou's Culture*)，上海：上海人民出版社，1988。

Chen Mengjia 陈梦家：《殷虚卜辞综述》，北京：科学出版社，1956。

Chinese-English Dictionary《汉英词典》，北京外国语学院英语系《汉英词典》编写组编，北京：商务印书馆，1980。

Claiborne，Robert. *The Birth of Writing.* Nederland，Time-life International，1974。

Da，Shiping *and* Shen，Guanghai　达世平，沈光海：《古汉语常用字字源字典》，上海：上海书局，1989。

Daniel，Glyn. *A Short History of Archaeology.* London：THAMES AND HUDSON Ltd.，1981.

Dawenkow. Xinshiqi Shidai muzang fajue baogao《大汶口——新石器时代墓葬发掘报告》(*Excavation report regarding neolithic grave finds in Dawenkow*)，北京：文物出版社，1974。

Dykstra，Andrew. *The Kanji ABC.* William Kaufmann，Inc. 1977.

Fagan，Brian M.（1）. *Quest for the Past.* Addison-Wesley Publishing Company，1978.

　—（2）. *People of the Earth.* Little Brown and Company，1980.

Fazzioli，Edoardo. *Chinese Calligraphy——From Pictograph to Ideogram. The History of 214 Essential Chinese / Japanese Characters.*

Gai，Shanlin 盖山林（1）：《阴山岩画》(*Petroglyphs in the Yinshan Mountains*)，北京：文物出版社，1986。

　—（2）：《乌兰察布岩画》(*Petroglyphs in the Wulanchabu Grassland*)，北京：文物出版社，1989。

Gao，Ming 高明：《古文字类编》(*Compilation of Chinese Paleographs*)，北京：中华书局，1980。

Gao Shufan 高树藩：《形音义综合大字典》，正中书局，中华民国七十三年增订五版。

Guo，Moruo *see* Kuo，Mo-jo.

He，Linyi 何琳仪：《战国文字通论》，北京：中华书局，1989。

Ho，Ping-ti 何炳棣. *The Cradle of the East.* The Chinese University of Hong Kong and the University of Chicago Press，1975.

Hu，Houxuan 胡厚宣（1）：《甲骨探史录》，北京：三联书店，1982。

　—（2）：《甲骨文与殷商史》，上海古籍出版社，1983。

Hu，Qiguang 胡奇光：《中国小学史》，上海：上海人民出版社，1987。

Jia Lanpo 贾兰坡. *Early Man in China*. Beijing：Foreign Languages Press，1980.

Kang，Yen 康殷 (1)：《汉字源流浅说（释例篇）》，北京：荣宝斋出版社，1979。
  —(2)：《说文部首》，北京：荣宝斋出版社，1980。
  —(3)：《古文字形发微》，北京：北京出版社，1990。
Karlgren，Bernhard（高本汉）(1). *Analytic dictionary of Chinese and Sino-Japanese. Paris，P. Geuthner*，1923.
  —(2). *Word families in Chinese*. Stockholm，1934.
  —(3). *The Chinese Language，an essay on its nature and history*. New York The Ronald Press Co. 1949.
  —(4). *Easy lessons in Chinese Writing*. Stockholm，Naturmetodens Sprakinstitut，1958.
Kato，Tunetaka and Yamada，Katumi 加藤常贤，山田胜美：《字源辞典》，角川书店，昭和四十七年初版。
Keightley，David N. *Sources of Shang History，the Oracle-Bone Inscription of Bronze Age China*. University of California Press，Berkeley and Los Angeles，1978，p281.
Kim，Jacob Chang-ui. *Pictorial Sino-korean Characters Fun with Hancha* 汉字学习. Hollym International Corp. Elizabeth New Jersey，USA and Seoul，Korea，1987.
Kuo，Mo-jo 郭沫若 (1)：《中国史稿》第一册，北京：人民出版社，1976。
  —(2)：《卜辞通纂》，北京：科学出版社，1983。

Li，Renpu 李仁溥：《中国古代纺织史稿》，岳麓出版社，1983。
Li，Xiaoding 李孝定：《甲骨文字集释》（*Explanations of the Oracle Bone Characters*），台北，1965，16 vol.
Li，Xueqin 李学勤 (1). *The Wonder of Chiense Bronzes*. Beijing：Foreign Languages Press，1980.
  —(2)：《古文字初阶》，北京：中华书局，1985。
Li，Yujie 李玉洁：《常用汉字形音义》，长春：吉林教育出版社，1990。
Lin，Yutang 林语堂：《当代汉英词典》*Chinese-English Dictionary of Modern Usage*. The Chinese University of Hong Kong，1972.
Lindqvist，Cecilia（林西莉）. *CHINA Empire of the Written Symbol*（汉字源流），translated from the Swedish by Joan Tate. harvill，Great Britain，1991.

Luo，Zhenyu 罗振玉：《三代吉金文存》，北京：中华书局，1983。（影印版，20 vol.）
Mao，Peiqi et al. 毛佩琦等：《岁月河山——图说中国历史》，上海：上海古籍出版社，1989。
Meng，Shikai 孟世凯：《甲骨学小词典》，上海：上海辞书出版社。
Needham，Joseph. *Science and Civilization in China*. Cambridge：Cambridge University Press，1954—. 李约瑟：《中国科学技术史》，北京：科学出版社，上海：上海古籍出版社，1990—。

Qinghai Liuwan《青海柳湾》，北京：文物出版社，1984。
Qiu Xigui 裘锡圭：《文字学概要》，北京：商务印书馆，1988。

Rawson，Jessica. *Ancient China，Art and Archaeology*. London：British Museum，1980.
Renfrew，Colin. *Archaeology and Language，The Puzzle of Indo-European Origins*. Penguin Books，1989.
Rong，Geng 容庚：《金文编》（*Compilation of Bronze Characters*），北京：中华书局，1985（影印本）。

Shirakawa, Shizuka 白川静：《文字逍遥》，东京：平凡社，1987。

Sun，Jingchen 孙景琛：《中国舞蹈史（先秦部分）》，文化艺术出版社，1983。

Sun，Yunhe 孙云鹤：《常用汉字详解字典》，福州：福建人民出版社。

Tang, Lan 唐兰 (1)：《中国文字学》，上海：上海古籍出版社，1979。

— (2)：《古文字学导论》，济南：齐鲁书社，1981（增订本）。

— (3)：《殷虚文字记》，北京：中华书局，1981。

Tian, Changwu *et al.*, *eds.* 田昌五主编：《华夏文明》第一集，北京：北京大学出版社，1987。

Vaccari, Oreste *and* Vaccari, Enko Elisa. *Pictorial Chinese-Japanese Characters* （汉字之母体），*A New and Fascinating Method to Learn Ideographs.* Vaccari's Languages Institute, Tokyo, 1968.

Wang, Tongyi 王同忆：《英汉词海》*The English-Chinese Word-Ocean Dictionary*，北京：国防工业出版社，1987。

Wang, Renshou [清]汪仁寿：《金石大字典》，天津市古籍书店影印出版，1982。

Wang，Dayou 王大有：《龙凤文化源流》，北京：北京工艺美术出版社，1987。

Wang，yuxin 王宇信 (1)：《建国以来甲骨文研究》，北京：中国社会科学出版社，1981。

— (2)：《甲骨学通论》，ibid，1989。

Wang，Zhuxi 王竹溪：《新部首大字典》，上海翻译出版公司 电子工业出版社联合出版，1988。

Webster's Word Histories. Merriam-Webster Inc. , Publishers. Springfield, Massachusetts.

Wen，Shaofeng *and* Yuan, Tingdong 温少峰，袁庭栋：《殷墟卜辞研究·科学技术篇》，成都：四川省社会科学院出版社，1983。

Wenke, Robert J. *Patterns in Prehistory.* New York. Oxford：Oxford University Press，1980.

Williamson，Leslie. *The Invention of Chinese Script.* England：Yi Publishing.

Wu, Cengde 吴曾德：《汉代画像石》，北京：文物出版社，1984。

Wu, Haokun *and* Pan, You 吴浩坤，潘悠：《中国甲骨学史》，上海：上海人民出版社，1985。

Wu，Shan 吴山：《中国新石器时代陶器装饰艺术》，北京：文物出版社，1982。

Wu，Zhao *and* Liu，Dongsheng 吴钊，刘东升：《中国音乐史略》，人民音乐出版社，1983。

Xi'an Banpo《西安半坡》(*Stone Age Village in Banpo, Xi'an*)，北京：文物出版社，1963。

Xin Zhongguo de kaogu faxian he yanjiu《新中国的考古发现和研究》(*Archaeological Excavation and Researches in New China*)，考古学专刊甲种第十七号，中国社会科学院考古研究所编著，北京：文物出版社，1984。

Xu Fancheng 徐梵澄 (F. C. Hsu). *An Analysis of the Chinese Language, An Etymological Approach.* Vol. 1：words.

Xu, Shen [汉]许慎：《说文解字》，北京：中华书局，1963（影印）。

Xu，Weijian 许伟建：《上古汉语通假字字典》，深圳：海天出版社，1989。

Xu, Zhongshu *et al.*, *eds.* 徐中舒主编(1)：《汉语古文字字形表》(*Compilation of different forms of early Chinese Characters*)，成都：四川人民出版社，1981。

— (2)：《甲骨文字典》(*The Dictionary of Oracle-Bone Characters*)，成都：四川辞书出版社，1988。

Yamada, Katumi 山田胜美：《汉字的语源》，角川书店，昭和五十一年初版。

Yu, Qiuyu 余秋雨：《华语情结》("*Complex*" *of Chinese Language*)，《文汇月刊》90/6，p. 45（停刊号）。

Yu, Xingwu 于省吾:《甲骨文字释林》，北京：中华书局，1979。

Yuyan wenzi guifan shouce《语言文字规范手册》(*A standard handbook of the Chinese Language and Writing*)，语文出版社编，北京：语文出版社，1991（增订本）。

Zhongguo gudai tu'an《中国古代图案》(*Chinese Ancient Design*)，北京纺织科学研究所编，北京：人民美术出版社，1979。

Zhongguo junshi shi《中国军事史》第一卷·兵器 (*History of the Chinese Military, Vol. 1 Weaponry*)，《中国军事史》编写组编，北京：解放军出版社，1983。

Zhou, Fagao *et al.*, *eds.* 周法高主编:《金文诂林》，(*Explanations of Bronge Characters*)，香港，1974—77 (19 Vol.)。

Zhu, Boxiong *et al.*, *eds.* 朱伯雄主编:《世界美术史》第一卷·原始美术，济南：山东美术出版社，1986。

Zhu, Di 朱狄:《原始文化研究》，北京：三联书店，1988。

Encyclopedia

The New Encyclopedia Britannica. 15th edition, Encyclopedia Britannica, Inc. Chicago, 1986.

The Encyclopedia Americana. International Ed. Danbury, Americana Corp., 1980.

Oxford Illustrated Encyclopedia. Vol. 1 The Physical World, Vol. 2 The Natural World. Oxford University Press, 1985.

Zhongguo dabaike quanshu《中国大百科全书》(*The China's Encyclopedia*)，中国大百科全书出版社，北京上海，1986。

Magazine

Kaogu《考古》月刊 (*Archaeology, monthly*)。

Wenwu《文物》月刊 (*Cultural Relics, monthly*)。

Kaogu yu Wenwu《考古与文物》(*Archaeology and Cultural Relics, monthly*)。

Yuyan Wenzixue《语言文字学》(*Study of Language and Writing, monthly*)，中国人民大学书报资料中心复印报刊资料，月刊。

Kejishi wenji《科技史文集》1—14 辑 (*Essays of the History of the Chiense Science and Technology*)，上海科技出版社。

Guwenzi yanjiu《古文字研究》(*Study of Paleographs*) 1—17 辑，中华书局编辑部等编，北京：中华书局，1981—。

INDEX FOR CHARACTERS

208

INDEX

Numerals in brackets refer to illustrations

责任编辑　周奎杰
封面设计　张大羽

汉字字源入门

王宏源　著

*

©华语教学出版社

华语教学出版社出版

(中国北京百万庄路 24 号)

邮政编码 100037

北京外文印刷厂印刷

中国国际图书贸易总公司发行

(中国北京车公庄西路 35 号)

北京邮政信箱第 399 号　邮政编码 100044

1993 年(16 开)第一版

1997 年第三次印刷

(汉英)

ISBN 7-80052-243-1/H · 240 (外)

04000

9-CE-2775P